# The Islamic War on Christians

Peter Riga

authorHOUSE®

*AuthorHouse™*
*1663 Liberty Drive*
*Bloomington, IN 47403*
*www.authorhouse.com*
*Phone: 1-800-839-8640*

*Published by AuthorHouse   07/05/2012*

*ISBN: 978-1-4772-0914-1 (sc)*
*ISBN: 978-1-4772-0915-8 (e)*

*Library of Congress Control Number: 2012908966*

# CONTENTS

# INTRODUCTION

It is with the greatest sorrow that I have written this book. Its conclusions are neither optimistic nor joyful. The result of years of research on the relationship between Islam and Christianity has brought me to this sorrowful conclusion: the original *jihad* begun by Mohammad is now continuing into the twenty first century in obedience to the demand or order of the Prophet: the whole world must be ruled by *sharia* - God's law. For Islam, the whole world is divided between the lands of Islam where *sharia* rules and lands of war where *sharia* does not rule and there is perpetual *jihad* between the two until the last day. That is exactly what Mohammad had in mind as he led his armies of conquest into some seventy two battles during his lifetime. He commanded his followers to continue this *jihad* until the whole world is subject to God's law of *sharia*. Only then can there be peace in the world.

Does this mean that all Muslims are violent and desire to suppress or subjugate the infidel by force and violence? By no means. But the reality remains that the holy books of Islam - the *Quran*, the *Hadith* - demand of every Muslim that he or she participate in *jihad* in one way or another. If a particular Muslim does not engage in violence or other efforts to bring this about, he or she is not a true Muslim. This *jihad* may be violent or non violent, depending on the strength of the Islamic community. A peaceful way is initiated when Muslims are a minority and without power known as Islamization. This means, first by not being absorbed into an alien culture and secondly, by slowly introducing Islamic mores and practices until Muslims are strong enough to impose full *sharia*. That may take centuries but the effort in this respect must be made by all Muslims.

If such conversion could come about in freedom, there would be no problem with Islam; every religion has the right to non violently try and convert to his faith which he or she considers the truth. There could be no problem with this because that is what freedom of religion is all about. But such is not and has never been the case in recent times with Islam. As Benedict XVI is constantly preaching, there can be and must not be any violence in religion. Each person as matter of conscience must be free to believe or not to believe as he or she sees fit without coercion or any threat of violence. Such is not the case in much of the Muslim world.

Alas this has not been the case with Islam today. Its history is one long history of violence, conquest and submission to Islam in the lands which they have conquered by force. That continues today throughout the world except in countries where Muslims are in a minority. It is only then that Muslims claim that they are a religion of peace. But as soon as their numbers increase to ten to twenty percent, demands are made on the state to live under *sharia*. The point of this small book is that we in the West must not allow this to happen under pain of losing our freedom as the fruits of a Judeo-Christian culture. That is the irony of Islam which is not only a religion but a political ideology as well since there is no separation of church/

state in Islam. The whole of life in every respect is contained in the *sharia*. That is also why Islam divides the world into two groups: lands of Islam where people are ruled by *sharia* and lands of war where *sharia* does not rule. War means precisely that, conquest by violence or non violent means (Islamization).

In addition, it must be noted once and for all that *sharia* (codification of the *Quran*) contradicts each and every value contained in western culture and in the United States Constitution. Its beliefs contradict western values at their very root: human dignity of every human being, separation of church and state, secular law administered by secular judges and an independent judicial system, equality of all people before the law, freedom of all to choose to believe or not (religious freedom) with no coercion by any group, religious or secular. Each of these values are contradicted by *sharia* so that the two cannot coexist in the same place at the same time. This makes dialogue between Christianity/Islam impossible unless both renounce the use of violence in the matter of religion. And that there be no deception which is permitted in Islam (*takiyyah*). A person cannot be a faithful American and a faithful Muslim and try to live by both forms of law at the same time. One must choose: freedom under the Constitution with Judeo-Christian values or *sharia* which denies these values we live by in the United States. There are ruses employed by Islam: when a minority they live by the laws of the land they are in. When strong enough, they must throw off secular law and adhere only to *sharia*. For this Muslims may employ *takiyyah* or deception or lies to the infidel in the interest of Islam. This is perhaps the greatest obstacle to any form of honest dialogue with Islam since we do not know when Muslims are truthful and when they are not. Religious freedom is not a Muslim value as we can see by even a short glance in the *Quran* (e.g. a person cannot leave Islam without a death sentence upon him or her). How can there be a genuine dialogue between those who believe in freedom of conscience and those who do not? Either one or the other must prevail. In the words of Abraham Lincoln 157 years ago: a nation cannot be half slave and half free.

That is the reason why I have written this small book: a warning of this danger, particularly to Christians who are persecuted all over the world. As long as Muslims adhere to the values of the *Quran*, dialogue is difficult if not impossible. The differences are radical (e.g. human rights, nature of violence in religion, the image each of us has of God, etc.). But is there any possibility of dialogue and peace with Islam and Muslims? Yes, but only if some very stringent rules are adopted, e.g. no violence in religion. There are areas of economic development, security, respect of each other that can be promoted by such dialogue. But there must be constant vigilance since the Islamic holy books are there like a loaded gun that may be taken up literally at any time by any Muslim who takes those texts seriously and literally. It is in this spirit that this book is written. In the words of Ronald Reagan - "trust but verify" - I want to trust but given the history of violence in Islam, I want to verify and be vigilant.

Houston, Texas
October 30, 2012

# CHAPTER 1

# THE GATHERING STORM

Now that six Muslims were apprehended before they could complete their *jihad* against United States soldiers at Fort Dix, New Jersey, killing as many of them as possible, it is time for some honest talk. While three of these men were illegal aliens who had overstayed their visas (not thought to be a serious violation), the other three seem to be United States citizens betraying their own country. This is not strange since Islam purports to be not only a universal religion which it is, but one nation, not divided into different states as in the West, but one Islamic nation, one Islamic community under the direction and rule of *sharia* (sacred Islamic law) and under one Califate or under the one successor of Mohammad whose work it is to unite and protect the Islamic community all over the world as well as to continue the original *jihad* against the infidels into the land of war, i.e. those lands not yet under the domination and rule of Islam. The *Quran* directly teaches that sooner or later the whole world will be under the rule of Islam and its sacred law. Most Muslims consider that time to be in the distant future while others of the so called fundamentalist variety, want to bring it about now by holy and violent *jihad*. It is holy war because its object is to obey the command of Allah to bring the whole world under the rule of God's holy law. For that, any means can be used.

This holy law of God (called *sharia*) has been dictated by God himself to Mohammad in a cave in Saudi Arabia in Arabic. The *Quran* and *sharia*, its law, are the incarnation of God himself - which must be obeyed literally and absolutely because it is God's very word which may not be evolved or forsaken on "reinterpreted" or changed in anyway. This law is God's law and must be obeyed in every area of life. The infidel on the other hand has enacted human laws and constitutions which must be eliminated because they stand in the way of God's will. This sacred law governs all phases of human life - there is no separation of church/state - from governance, to hygiene, to food, to relationship between men, women, infidels, to penal laws, to probate and court proceedings, etc. There is no impartial secular law applicable equally to all but only God's holy law applied and interpreted by the mullahs as in Iran and Sudan. One can plainly see how authentic Islam in the *Quran* is diametrically to the legal system and way of life (values) of the West: secular law, popular sovereignty, democracy, equality before the law, separation of religion from the state, secular courts, etc. all this is anathema to authentic Islam. There is a basic and radical difference between the two value systems (Islam and the West). In the land of war (lands not yet subject to Islam and its holy law), Muslims are to live, convert by example if possible but by violence if necessary, so as to bring these lands under

1

the domination of Islam. Those who resist are infidels who declare war on Islam and who therefore may be killed any where, by any means (this is the view of Bin Laden which appears on tapes and videos put out by him. And since there is no central authority in Islam to spell out authentic Islamic doctrine, Bin Laden's views of Islam are as valid as any other view of Islam.) One must understand this when one hears Muslims say that Islam is a religion of peace. It is a religion of peace only after the whole world follows God's will and comes under the rule of Islam - why else do you think they call non Muslim lands, the land of war?

None of the men seized in New Jersey had any orders from Al Qaeda or were associated with any other fundamentalist group. They were plain Muslims who were following the basic command of the *Quran* to continue the *jihad* begun by Mohammad himself back in the 7th century.

One has only to read the *Quran* for oneself to discover this. *Jihad* is a divine command because the whole world is destined to come under the rule of God's law not human law. There are injunctions in the *Quran* on how to bring this about which do not exclude violence and the killing of Jews, infidels and Christians. It is very unpleasant reading as opposed, say, to the New Testament where there isn't a word of force or violence to spread the Christian faith and the commands of Jesus.

Here is the very unpleasant reality which few in the U.S. are willing to face: there are not two kinds of Muslims, one fundamentalist and violent, the other moderate and peaceful. There is only one kind of Muslim divided into two commitments: one who takes the *Quran* seriously and lives it (like the six Muslims captured) and the other who does not - a kind of cafeteria Muslim who picks and chooses which doctrines he will follow and which he will not.

By cafeteria Muslim I mean one who postpones final universal domination by Islam of the whole world for end time so as to be able to live in peace with infidels. Thus we find law abiding, peaceful Muslims who obey the law and live their faith as unobtrusively as possible. They want to get along so they postpone and place all this Quranic teaching to the indefinite future. The fundamentalist Muslim wants that domination now even by violent means.

The great danger is that so called moderate Muslims can become fundamentalist in the blink of an eye. It is Islam itself that is the danger to the U.S. and the West because we are engaged not in a war on terrorism (that's absurd) but in a religious-theological war of radically different values which can only result in the death and defeat of one or the other.

Here is the logic of Islam in four very simple propositions:

- Allah commands that the whole world come under the rule of his holy law - *sharia*
- Allah's followers are absolutely bound by this holy law and must strive to bring it about by peaceful means if possible but by violent means if necessary
- Followers like Bin Laden, the Wahabis, Al Qaeda and other fundamentalist Islamic groups who want to bring this about by violent means cannot be shown to be incorrect
- Therefore the war on terrorism is not one on terrorism but on an authentic interpretation of Islam whose numbers are in the millions all over the world. And

growing. Peaceful Muslims may turn on us infidels at any time "they get religion." These six captured Muslim terrorists are a perfect example.

Here is our real problem, one so frightening in its connotations, that few are willing to address it honestly. Until we do, we stand in mortal danger of our own destruction.

# CHAPTER 2

# WHAT THIS WAR IS ALL ABOUT

IT IS IMPORTANT TO know just what kind of war we are engaged in. Too many Americans who want or demand withdrawal from Iraq (including many religious leaders) do not seem to realize that that is exactly what our Islamic enemy wants. This is not a war like other wars so that by defeating an army, declaring a victory and go home victorious as in WWI and II, we may thereby end it. We got a little glimpse of this kind of war in Vietnam which was conducted by insurgents, terror and hiding among the civilian population. But the difference between the two wars is radically different.

This war is a global war of religion which seeks to establish the Califate - successor of Mohammad - in order to subject the whole world to *sharia,* the Islamic holy law, *by any means necessary.* The enemy in this war can only be defeated by death which is gladly accepted in this global struggle called *jihad.* This started with Mohammad out from Arabia who conquered mostly Christian countries of North Africa, Byzantium, the Baltic States, parts of India and as far away as China and Indonesia. In the West, Islam extended its conquest of other Christian nations through Spain and into France while in the East, they went as far as Turkey and parts of Bulgaria, Hungary, Russia and Azerbaijan. Islamic conquest also reached important parts of Africa (Somalia, Egypt, Ivory Coast, Sudan, Nigeria, Angola, etc.). All these conquests began by Mohammad himself who led his armies into at least seventy two battles known as holy war or *jihad* which is incumbent on all Muslims. This kind of religion was/is ongoing and is incumbent on every Muslim when possible and by every means possible including terror and subversion. This is taught by the *Quran* itself.

The major obstacle to this on going conquest by the sword - this has somewhat changed by using democratic procedures as in Europe and the United States - is the great Satan called the U.S. which once defeated, will open up the whole world to submission to Islam to be ruled by the holy law (*sharia*). This kind of war may ebb and flow but fundamentally it is a command of the *Quran* itself on a world wide basis which can never be halted or given up. It is an essential part of Islamic teaching. That is why removal of American troops from Iraq and Afghanistan will not only not bring us peace; but will simply strengthen this enemy as it takes more and more territories and subjects them to Muslim law. Thus *jihad* is a radical, expansionist, totalitarian ideology that seeks to establish global Islamic states ruled by Islamic law. This kind of war can be given up only by the death of Muslims because it is a struggle to the death which cannot be resolved by armistice or declaration. No other religion has such an objective or means to accomplish that objective. The only concession Muslims can make in this regard are temporary treaties to give Muslims time to build up their forces to attack Jews, Crusaders (Christians) and infidels. These groups - as well as all infidels - will then have three choices:

- accept Islam in conversion
- pay the tax of submission - *jizya* - as second class citizens
- or death

There will be no other choices open to non Muslims as they seek global conquest of the world.

The most influential institution in Sunni Islam, Cairo's Al-Azhar University defines *jihad* as "war against non Muslims." It spells out the nature of this war in specific terms: "The caliph makes war upon Jews [and] Christians.... until they become Muslim or pay the non Muslim poll tax (*jizya*)." Or in the words of Osama Bin Laden that "killing Americans and their allies - both civilians and military personnel - is a commandment for every individual Muslim who can do this, in any country in which he can do this." Does that sound as if we will have any kind of peace if and when we withdraw our troops from Iraq? Or listen to the words of Sheik Abd Al-Aziz Qari, preacher in the mosque in Medina: "When we say that annihilating the infidel forces is a divine decree, it means that it is an immutable, valid law and a constant principle that does not change with time, place, people and circumstances...."

There are other trouble spots which Americans think, if resolved, will bring peace. Take the Palestinian question. This land belongs to Islam because God gave it to Muslims which cannot be returned to infidels once conquered. That was done in the eighth century. Therefore there can be no peace with Israel (Muslim law) until Israel is destroyed and its people dispersed. That is in the very constitution of Hamas and is accepted by Muslims the world over. Any negotiations can only be temporary in nature until Islamic forces can be built up to defeat and destroy the Jews. The President of Iran, Ahmadinejad, has said this time and again, even before the United Nations which did nothing even as one of its members (Israel)was threatened with extinction. Why else is Iran building up a nuclear arsenal and a delivery system? All this is being done in order to fulfill the promises which people like the President of Iran are making. Not taking him seriously is exactly like we did not take Hitler seriously in the 1930's. As a survivor of the Holocaust put it, if your enemy threatens to kill you, believe him! Thus in summary, it is useless to try and negotiate peace with the Palestinians because of their Islamic ideology.

None of this is hidden or secretive. These intentions and threats are there in various books, speeches by prominent Muslims and indeed in the very sacred texts of the *Quran* and can he heard in almost any mosque on Friday during the sermons of the imams. There are none so blind as those who do not want to see. This is what this war is all about!

It is useless to give quote after quote to verify any of this. It is right there in the *Quran*, the messages of Bin Laden, Maldudi, Ahmadinejad, Sheik Nasses ibn Hamed, Qari, Sheik Ahmed Abu Halabiya, Hassan Nasrallah - and many, many more. It is absolutely astounding that the American people who are being told to their face about the global intent of their enemy day in and day out, do not consider this a great danger and no more important than other criminal acts. Of course that was the thought of the Byzantine emperors who were conquered and subverted by Muslims and who no longer exist today. If it were not like courageous men like Charles Martel, Leo the lion hearted, Jan Sobieski, various popes like Urban II, we would today be speaking Arabic and worshiping Allah in mosques all over Europe. We are beginning to see this again all over Europe as Muslims occupy Europe through large birth rates and immigration as opposed to the dwindling population of Europe.

This is truly a global threat from a religion which seeks the death of infidels or at least their conversion or submission - even by force of arms. This is what this war is all about and Americans in general do not seem to realize the danger they are being subjected to at the very core of who and what they are. Their anti war stance today (including that of religious leaders like the American Catholic bishops) is truly a form of national suicide. Never in history has a whole people demanded not just their own defeat by withdrawing from this war; rather they are demanding their own national suicide.

# CHAPTER 3

# ERRONEOUS PRONOUNCEMENTS AT CAIRO BY PRESIDENT OBAMA

As a Christian, I have seen no objections from Christian sources to some of the statements which President Obama tried to make in his opening to the Islamic world in Cairo, Egypt in June, 2009. That opening was doomed from the beginning. Such criticisms are not objections to the President's opening to the Islamic world; rather they are aimed at the fact that no Christian would ever make such remarks. In fact, many of the President's remarks are contrary to Christian beliefs and should be confronted forthrightly particularly by Christian religious writers and authors. The President has often claimed to be a Christian (to which he was converted as an adult) but these remarks at Cairo betray a fundamental ignorance of Christianity *vis-a-vis* Islam. There is a doctrine in Shia theology that in defense of Islam and for its protection, a believer may lie to an infidel. This is a most dangerous doctrine since it poisons all dialogue. Be that as it may, no Christian would make the following remarks made by the President at Cairo as contrary to Christian faith. The statements made by the President actually deny Christian faith. That is why his words were enthusiastically received by the Muslim audience. Any dialogue with Islam must be based on openness and truth. Otherwise there is no dialogue.

*Reference was made by the President to the "Holy" Quran* No Christian would refer to that book as "holy" when it contains so much violence, killing, hatred of Jews and infidels. That book refers to Jews as descendants of pigs and monkeys and all infidels are destined to Hell unless they convert to Islam. In fact, the word 'infidel' means filth and refuse and that is what Muslims consider the President to be because he is not a Muslim. There are some 450 references in the *Quran* calling for the killing of Jews and infidels. Muslims are called upon to kill Jews wherever they find them. How such a text can be called "holy" by any Christian whose religion is one of love, even for enemies is simply beyond all belief. There is not a word of hatred much less killing of enemies in the New Testament and the teachings of Jesus. In fact, Christ calls upon his followers to love enemies and to do good to those who hate them in order to be like God, their Father, who loves all his children. Christians refer to the Bible as the Holy Bible because its God is a God of mercy, love and compassion to all God's children. In fact, in Christianity, God is love. The God of Islam is hardly any of this as any examination of the *Quran* will reveal. The Islamic God hates infidels as enemies and wishes them ill. This may not be ecumenical to say but the God of Jesus and the God of Mohammad are so radically different as to be two separate Gods unreconcilable to each other. We in the West have become too politically correct to admit to any of this so we use bromides such as "Islam is a religion of peace" in spite of the fact that Islam has been at war and conquest for over fourteen hundred years.  One need only read the *Quran* and the *New Testament* and compare.  Whatever else Islam is, it is not a religion of peace because it divides the whole world into the house of Islam and the house of war (where *sharia* does not rule).  War is not peace unless we want to pervert language..

"I have known Islam on three continents before coming to the region *where it was first revealed*," said the President.   No Christian believes that the *Quran* (cf. *supra*) was ever revealed by God to Mohammad. Whatever Muslims believe is fine and we must respect that but no Christian believes that the *Quran* is a revelation from God. Were that the case, then it would contradict the whole Christian notion of God as essentially love while Islam purports to know nothing of God. . You cannot have both. That may be and is a Muslim belief but such a belief is foreign to any Christian. There are parts of the *Quran* that are beautiful and spiritual, but as a whole it cannot be seen as 'revealed' by any Christian. The only "revelations" for any Christian are the books of the Bible and only these; and Jesus as the visibility of the invisible God; we believe that these books  are the inspired words of God and also the creation of man. They are both word of God and word of man. To hold that such "revelation" as contained in the *Quran* is from God is to see God as Muslims see God, that is,  as a vindictive, murderous and vengeful God who calls on his followers to kill those who do no believe. Muslims may believe this but this is utterly foreign to Christianity and the Christian God as revealed in Jesus.  For a Christian, the *Quran* is not revelation but a pure Arabic concoction sprinkled with citations borrowed from the Bible. For the Christian, the *Quran* was neither revealed nor inspired by God.  This may be a hard truth but it is the truth as Christians see it and should not be denied by any Christian.

*Referring to Mohammad as "peace be upon him"* is an Islamic phrase and custom used by no Christian. Given the history of Mohammad, his killings of his Jewish enemies and hostages, his child marriages, his leading of his armies in seventy two battles, his killing of Christians, his admonitions to violence and death,  his slaughter of innocents and rejoicing in the death of his enemies, such a phrase would be anathema to any Christian.  No Christian would even recite such a phrase let alone believe it. To do so is to be blind to the reality of who and what Mohammad was. There are perhaps other words to describe Mohammad and his deeds but "peace" upon him is not one of them. For Mohammad, it is the peace of death for all Jews and infidels unless they convert to Islam.  Before the historical evidence about Mohammad, a Christian may only maintain a respected silence at the very most so as not to offend.  But at least we should not say what is not true.

*The number of Muslims in America is put by the President at "nearly seven million"* That is pure nonsense and all the polls of Muslims in America reach no more than two million.  This is Islamic propaganda put out by various Islamic groups in America to magnify their political importance and influence. This statement is hardly worthy of the President of the United States who should have known better.  It was good of the President to show the Islamic world that Muslims can come to America and live and worship in peace and freedom - something hardly present in the Muslim world where Christians are killed and their churches attacked.

*Worst of all, the President refers to Moses, Mohammad and Jesus praying together in*

*Jerusalem* For Muslims, all three are dead prophets while the fundamental and basic belief of Christians is not that Jesus is dead but that he is very much alive in and through his death and resurrection in what is known as the pascal mystery. And only Jesus. The other two are as dead as stones. That is the very core of Christian belief which no Christian can deny and still remain a Christian. The doctrine of the pascal mystery alone makes the radical difference between Islam and Christianity: the Christ who is the Son of God, dead and resurrected is anathema to Islam as blasphemy. This is a hard saying for Muslims to hear but it must be honestly said so that Muslims can understand who we are. To associate the living Christ with the dead Mohammad and Moses is a direct denial of the Christian faith. And to associate the living and resurrected Christ as the equal with Mohammad and Moses who are dead as stone is the supreme insult to Christian belief. The President told all this as he recounted the Muslim story of Isra when Jesus, Moses and Mohammad joined in prayer. For a Christian, that never happened. According to Islam, all three are dead prophets whereas Christians believe in the living Christ risen from the dead who conquered death for all who believe in him. The other two are stone dead. Not Christ. This reference to Isra is a denial and distortion of Christian faith and would not be repeated by Christians precisely because it is false.

There are still other misquotes from the *Quran*. "The Holy Koran" said the President, "teaches that whoever kills an innocent, it is as if he killed all mankind; and whoever saves a person, it is as if he has saved all mankind." The President studiously avoided the very next passage (5: 33) which mandates punishment for those whom Muslims do not regard as innocent, i.e. for those who fight against Allah and Mohammad. The President went on to quote the *Quran* (9: 119) that supposedly calls for inter-religious tolerance: "Be conscious of God and always speak the truth." But the passage continues, "O ye who believe! Fight those of the unbelievers whoa re near to you and let them find harshness in you, and know that Allah is with those who keep their duty [unto him] (9: 123). This is hardly inter-religious tolerance. The problem is this: how do you trust a man wanting better relations with Muslims and Islam, who misquotes the *Quran* so as to ingratiate himself to the Muslim world? If the "Holy Koran' mandates *jihad* against non Muslims, how can any good will from Americans be of any effect?

There were other profound non religious errors made by the president to ingratiate himself to the Muslim world but which were nonetheless not true. It was not Islam but the Greeks who invented algebra; it was the Chinese who gave us the compass not Islam and it was Johannes Gutenberg who created the wooden printing press and not Islam. These are errors which Islamic propaganda might give us but certainly not from an educated man like the President of the United States who should know much better about these things. Obama distorted history in order to ingratiate himself to the Muslim world. True dialogue does not engage in lies and untruths no matter how much we want retrenchment with the Islamic world. Anything that is based on anything but truth is bound to fail.

At this point, it is irrelevant whether President Obama is a covert Muslim or not. That really is not my concern. My concern involves the things he says about Islam *as a Christian*, which may seem true coming from some Islamic propaganda machine right here in America but hardly uttered out of a mouth of a believing Christian which Obama purports to be. No Christian would utter such phrases because he would consider them utterly untrue. One can be respectful without betraying one's whole system of belief which is what the President did in his speech to the Muslim world in Cairo on June 5, 2009. Perhaps that is the reason why in many months as President, we have seen him go to church only once during Easter. That is neither here nor there as proof; but it is or should be an indication of something to the Christians in the United States. Obama is hardly a religious Christian but the statements he made during his talk to Muslims in Cairo on June 5, 2009 are and remain basically anti Christian in the mouth of any Christian. They are simply not true and some one should say it loud and clear.

What could Obama have said to the Muslim world? All or any combinations of the following: That we have no desire to be at war with Islam; that we will defend our culture and our freedoms; that we will continue to have a strong military to defend our freedom and our interests (Muslims respect the strength of the strong horse); that we can help the Islamic world economically to develop themselves from the poverty in which much of the Muslim world is mired; that Muslims are welcomed to the United States as long as they do not seek to subvert our values; that there must be no violence in religion. These are basic truths for which we stand and we will fight to save them. The President should have pointed out how many times the United States has come to the aid of the Muslim world after earthquakes, tsunamis and other disasters; and how many times the United States has come to save Muslim lives in Somalia, Iraq, Bosnia and Darfur while spending its treasure and the lives of some of the best of its young..

There must be, finally, mutual respect for American freedom as we have for Islamic values which are different from ours. One simply cannot not become the other. That is what a super power should say to the whole world, the Muslim world included.. Muslims admire strength. As Bin Laden put it: between a strong horse and a weak horse, people will choose the strong horse. We are that strong horse and any attempt to change the American value system will be met with great force.

# CHAPTER 4

# ON THE NATURE OF RELIGIOUS FREEDOM: A COMPARISON WITH ISLAM

Perhaps the greatest contrast between Islam's *sharia* (religious law) and the Christian West is the basic human right of religious freedom. *Sharia* in fact does not hold to this basic human right inherent in every human person while the West *via* Christianity, does. How to reconcile the two? Is it even possible?

Islam's sacred law (*sharia*) holds that one has only one real right and freedom and that is to accept and submit to Islam. Everything else in the life of the believer is determined by *sharia*, socially, economically, sexually, militarily. Thus in the words of Afghanistan's Supreme Court Justice Fazi Hadi Shinnari, *Sharia* rejects three crucial freedoms so valued in the West: the right of expression, the right of religious freedom and equality of the sexes. He might have added the right of freedom of association and speech since that freedom is premised on the freedom of expression and belief. Yet this Islamic jurist was quite correct in associating all three rights because as we shall see in a moment, they are interdependent with the right of religious freedom holding the key to the rest because it is the font and origin of all other rights. The jurist cited these rights because they are denied in Islam and *sharia*

In fact, there can be no political freedom without religious freedom. Religious freedom belongs both to the individual (principally) as well as to the group. The religious group has the right to teach/preach freely, build places of worship and education, propagate itself and rule itself by its own internal rites and laws and announce publicly to all what it considers to be the truth, God's revelation, salvation, word, etc. Those who desire to listen are free to accept or reject this teaching and anyone can freely leave the group at any time for any reason for which he need give to no one. One has the basic right to criticize any religious belief. The group may not punish that person politically for leaving the group or deny him/her his/her political rights and freedoms. One of the great flaws and errors of Christianity in the past was the persecution and punishment of heretics by the use of the secular power to achieve this end. This was clearly erroneous because God does not force; neither may the Christian. The church may use its own form of punishment (e.g. excommunication, shunning, expulsion from the group, etc.) according to its own laws and decrees on its own constituents. But never by violence or coercion. We have long since evolved from this basic denial of religious freedom in the West whereas most of Islam (because of its non separation of church/state) has not. The reason is separation of church and state which is unknown in Islam. That is why there can be no religious freedom in Islam.

One of the real problems for Islam is that this denial of religious freedom is contained in the *sharia* itself which it believes to be the direct, immediate word of God which cannot evolve, allegorize or be reinterpreted. Christianity's evolution in this respect in the modern period is really going back to the teachings of Christ himself in the New Testament who never coerced or used force in belief but left all free to accept or reject his message with no violent consequences. The church followed this for the first three hundred years of its existence and only later became involved with the state after Constantine who gave the church freedom after the year 313. The church has evolved from that deviation in the past hundred years. Today she is the foremost defender of religious freedom in the world today.

Most importantly is the notion of religious freedom as a human right which is inherent in the very nature of the human person as an individual. In fact, religious freedom is the most basic of all freedoms and is their font and source. Without religious freedom, the individual is held captive by other ideologies, state power or by religion itself. *Sharia* essentially is a denial of religious freedom and does not recognize it as an inherent human right. According to Islam, one is free only to believe in and submit to God's revelation - Islam and the *Quran* - and all those who do not are infidels condemned to death both in this life and in the next. Force may be used against infidels who reject Islam who may be attacked and killed (*jihad*). In fact, the *Quran* itself explicitly says that if any Muslim leaves Islam and is converted to another religion, he must be killed.

If the people who do not accept Islam are people of the book (Jews, Christians, Zoroastrians) they may worship in their own faith but only if they agree to the status of *dhimmitude* and pay the tax of submission to Islam as protection for living in Islamic lands. In other words, as long as they agree to be second class citizens in every respect under Muslims with all the disabilities foisted upon them by the *Quran* and *sharia*. This is a diminished form of religious freedom and as we shall see, is not religious freedom at all and in fact, is its denial.

Religious freedom is the source of all other freedoms. If one has religious freedom as a basic freedom, then it follows that one has the following rights as necessary corollaries:

*Freedom Of Association* In this freedom, I can freely choose with whom and where I shall worship, organize, listen to, etc. I may not be forbidden by state power to separate myself from a particular group whose teaching I reject or accept; nor can I be forbidden to join, be with and associate with any religious group which I consider true, revealed, advantageous in every respect, satisfying, joyful, fulfilling, etc. Religious freedom guarantees freedom of association with others of my choosing (and who also have the freedom to accept or to reject me). Muslims are told to make friends only with Muslims and never with unbelievers who are filth.

*Separation And Independence From The Power Of The State* The state or the secular power may not impose any system of religious belief because that is beyond its competence. The state has no power to force any belief, to promote or finance belief, to directly aid any belief as belief, to prosecute any belief unless it harms the good order of civil society. Religious freedom as an inherent human right must be respected by the state in law. Religious freedom is a guarantee of freedom *vis-a-vis* the state and any other religious group which may not use the secular power to enforce its beliefs on others. In other words, the only power any religious group has, negatively, is to be free of any coercive power of the state as to its beliefs and practices unless injurious to the common good and, positively, to freely appeal to others by its example and words to adhere and be converted to its beliefs and rituals but only if these others freely accept or reject that religious teaching, authority, doctrines, etc. Indirectly, religious freedom guarantees separation of church/state since the religious power may not use the secular power to enforce, forbid, propagandize or otherwise directly aid any religion. The state may not favor one religion over another or religion over non-religion because it does not have the competence to do so; and because it must respect the inherent right of religious freedom in each person. This must be guaranteed by law. All this in all respects is contrary to *sharia* for which there is no basic human right of religious freedom inherent in the human person. There is only the human right to believe in Islam and to submit to Allah's holy law.

All this is contrary to *sharia* for which there is no basic human right of religious freedom inherent in the human person. There is no separation of church and state which is one in Islam. Such power can enforce the Islamic faith. If it is not in *sharia* it does not exist. The Muslim person alone is a full person and infidels are not full persons in law and in court. Even Muslims are restricted because they may never leave Islam under penalty of death. There is also basic inequality between man and woman in Islam.

*Freedom Of Belief* This may be translated as the freedom of self determination which belongs exclusively to the human person as a basic right of freedom itself. Freedom means the right to find who one is, the purpose and meaning of life, the direction my life will take - or simply to reject this whole search for one's truth and direction and give one's life over to the pursuit of materialism, pleasure, consumerism, sexual satisfaction, etc. Herein lies real freedom which is simply another way of describing religious freedom. I am free to find meaning in my life i.e. my own religion which is guaranteed by law and the state and which responds to these basic questions. This is inherently an individual act and right which no one may exercise for me. This is denied in *sharia*. Only a Muslim has freedom precisely because he believes in Islam, the only true religion. To reject Islam is to reject God and to reject God is inherently evil for which the infidel deserves death and eternal damnation. That is why the infidel must be killed or if he is a person of the book, to live in a state of *dhimmitude* and pay the submission tax.

*Freedom Of Expression And Speech* Religious freedom implies the right to search, to inquire as to what religion I will follow *vel non*. That being so, I must have the right to freely speak, dialogue, exchange ideas with others in order to fulfill my right of religious freedom. Religious freedom is not found by being silent and mute; it must be spoken about in an exchange of ideas, views, respect with others. Only later on did this freedom develop into political free speech and still later, into commercial free speech. In Islam, there can be no legitimate criticism of Islam/Mohammad. In Muslim countries this is punished by blasphemy laws which can mean imprisonment or even death. This attempt at silencing any criticism of Islam is being pushed in the United Nations and has partially succeeded here in the United States. In America, to criticize Islam has become politically incorrect.

*Freedom Of The Press* Each person has the right to read freely and to have access to reading and other educational materials, to be informed about religion, philosophy, ideas, ideologies so that I can make up my own mind as to what I will follow, adhere to or respect in religion and political life. I must have access to such material - including the Internet - supplied by a free press so that I can learn, discourse, dialogue, exchange, etc. Freedom of the press is found here. This is hardly the case in Muslim countries. Any book that contradicts Islam is seized and burnt. Muslims are succeeding in this country to have books criticizing Islam seen as Islamaphobic and hate literature even when it quotes the *Quran* itself. This is for the West to admit to a form of *dhimmitude* out of fear of violence from Muslims, e.g. the Danish cartoons which produced so much violence and mayhem by Muslims all over the world.

*Freedom And Equality Of The Sexes* Since religious freedom adheres to the nature of every person as a basic right, this means that the sexes are equal in this search for religious meaning and expression in one's life. There is no superior/inferior status here. Implied in religious freedom therefore is the radical equality of the sexes to search, believe, respect, accept, read, reject, etc. It is the same for man and woman. This really implies a radical equality of men and women at the deepest level and which is at the source of women's other political, social and economic rights. Religious freedom really guarantees the radical equality of the sexes as its foundation from which all other rights of women flow. There is no equality of the sexes in Islam. Men may divorce at will but not women; men may take four wives but not women; husbands may beat their wives; the testimony of a woman is less than a man in court; there must be four male witnesses for rape or the woman is killed as an adulterer; a daughter is to receive less in heritage than a son; in case of divorce there is no alimony and all minor children are given to the male; a male Muslim may marry an infidel but a Muslim woman cannot; men may travel as they wish but a woman must have permission of her husband to leave the home and be accompanied by husband or male relatives. Young girls are mutilated by cutting off their clitoris to guarantee virginity before marriage. Does this sound like equality?

**Conclusion** One can now clearly see why religious freedom is so crucial to true freedom and democratic government. Anything that diminishes religious freedom diminishes all other rights as well. The law must guarantee this basic right to every person-citizen under penalty of being tyrannical and oppressive as are countries like Iran, northern Nigeria, North Korea, Vietnam, China, Pakistan, Saudi Arabia and Sudan. No one may even practice any religion but Islam in Saudi Arabia. Most of these nations are governed by *sharia* and not by a respect for human rights, democracy and freedom. In these countries, no law may pass if it contradicts *sharia* even in the new constitutions of Iraq and Afghanistan. In both countries, a Muslim who converts to another religion may be put to death legally. That is also why many women in Iraq were very disturbed when it was thought that Islam would be *the* source of law and not *a* source of law in their constitution. Why? Consider any of the above mentioned disabilities of women in Islam. One should note that those countries that have no religious freedom and therefore have no other freedoms which results in Islamo-fascism in law and in government as has already happened in Iran. In fact such rights do not exist in those countries under *sharia*. Because religious freedom is the foundation and source of all other rights (association, speech, press, separation of church/state) all other political and human rights are absent from these countries, all in the name of Islam! There are no real independent human rights under *sharia*.

The heart of the difference between Islam's basic law (*sharia*) and the West (which is at the heart of the present war on terrorism) is the very concept and reality of religious freedom as a basic right inherent in the nature of every person. Religious freedom is the foundation and source of all other rights and freedoms and without it, these other rights are either absent or questionable.

The basic question of the war on Islamic terrorism is this and only this, *"Does religious freedom exist as a basic human right for every person?"* The question is simple as well as its response. The West's answer is an emphatic 'yes.' That of *sharia* is an emphatic 'no.' We are fighting to guarantee that right for ourselves and for others. This implies a great difficulty in relation to those who take *sharia* seriously and devoutly. Such people cannot be true Democrats nor authentic citizens of the United States because the basis of the American proposition is the human right of religious freedom guaranteed to every human person irrespective of religion, race, nationality or color. If you do not accept that, you cannot be a true and loyal American; and it is difficult to understand how a devout Muslims living by *sharia* could be a loyal American. This is a terrible thing to say but it is true for one who seriously holds on to *sharia* as the basic law. Politicians in America refuse to admit it and the average American is ignorant of it. To even mention any of this is to be accused of racial hatred and Islamaphobia. It is neither because all this is the truth and it is the truth alone that can make us free.

**Special Note** This study should put to rest all talk about Islamic radicals who hijacked Islam. No one has hijacked Islam! Given the implications of this study on religious freedom, there can no longer be any doubt

– that Islam at its core is incompatible with western values of tolerance and religious freedom.

– Those Muslims who live in western nations are to be viewed as potentially subversive of the western values of religious freedom - core of the western experience,

– This shocking revelation poses a real problem for multiculturalism - that one culture and its values are as good as any other. This is profoundly dangerous and subversive of the notion of religious freedom. It is impossible to juxtapose the Islamic and the western view of religious freedom. They are profoundly antagonistic and cannot exist with each other. Either one or the other will and must prevail. The West does not seem capable of fighting to preserve its own culture.

– Our leaders must stop all the nonsense of "Islam is a religion of peace." At its core, Islam is the mortal enemy of western values, particularly of religious freedom. The real problem in the words of B. Lewis is that we no longer know who we are so how can we fight to preserve what we no longer hold? This moral confusion will lead to the triumph of Islam who holds no such confusion.

# CHAPTER 5

# THE ORIGIN OF TERRORISM IS ISLAM ITSELF

After Fort Hood, after Flight 253 over Detroit and after the attempted car bombing in Times Square by an American citizen, the dots should be connected back to Islam itself as a violent and conquering religion. Even in the face of overwhelming evidence that Malik Nadal Nasan of the Fort Hood massacre was a Muslim *jihadist* engaged in an act of *jihadist* terrorism against the United States, commentators and pundits still insisted on attributing the attack to aberrational religion or psychological reasons or stress. We even have a government report that says that Nasan was a deviant Muslim just as there are deviants in other religions. It is truly remarkable that this Fort Hood report compares Islam with the violence of other religions. Absolutely remarkable. . Even when Nasan's religion became the front and center evidence which clearly showed the influence of that religion, the conclusion (made ever since 9/11) was that Nasan was a deviant Muslim who distorted Islam for his own twisted purposes. Never mind that he began his attack yelling "Allah Akbar." On the contrary, Nasan understood perfectly well the nature of Islam and obtained all his incentives from the *Quran* and from the paradigmatic example of Mohammad as well as from the fourteen hundred year history of Islam. His communication with AlQaeda members via emails was well known to the authorities. All this shows that Islam is a religion of violence and conquest against the infidel who refuses submission ("Islam") to God's holy law of *sharia* at least for those who take these texts seriously and literally. It is the western inability or unwillingness to understand the nature, practices, history and texts of Islam that is so dangerous today. We thereby deny that it is Islam itself in its holy texts that is the unique source of terrorism.

Terrorism is a technique not an end and it is absurd to call this a "war on terrorism." There is no such thing. It is a war of Islamic terrorism because the violence issues from the nature and teaching of Islam itself commanding *jihad* against unbelievers. On December 8, 1941, it would have been absurd if President Roosevelt had urged Congress to declare war on sneak attacks; it was the sneak attack of the Japanese Empire against whom war was to be declared.

The *Quran* is so full of commands from Allah to kill infidels, Jews and Polytheists (Christians) that it is difficult to choose only a few such texts. We must first of all understand that for Muslims the *Quran* is the very word of God come directly from heaven, recited (i.e. Islam) to Mohammad which was later written down since Mohammad was illiterate. This word of God is in Arabic which must be accepted literally without allegory, without a parabolic sense or hyperbole or any other form of rational literary interpretation. It must be accepted literally without any rational interpretation. Moreover later texts in the *Quran* may supercede the earlier, peaceful texts composed while Mohammad was trying to make converts at Medina (mostly of Jews and Christians). When they refused conversion, Allah commanded violent *jihad* against them. So Mohammad himself killed thousands of unbelievers including a whole tribe of Jews who refused conversion. This is an absolute truth. Once you realize that, we must try to understand the nature of this religion born from and continued through history through these 'holy' books. That is quite easy for anyone who wants to take the trouble to read those texts which cannot be changed or allegorized. It is here that the obfuscation begins with bromides like "Islam is a religion of peace" when it is just the opposite. Here are seven examples taken directly from the *Quran* which show the nature of God's commandments:

"Then when the sacred months have passed, then kill the *Mustorikan* (the unbelievers of Allah, idolatries, polytheists, pagans) wherever you find them and capture them and besiege them, and prepare for them each and every ambush" *Sura 9: 5*

"Fight against those who believe not in Allah" *Sura 9: 29*

"So, when you meet those who disbelieve smite their necks, tell when you have killed and wounded many of them, then bind a bond firmly" *Sura 47: 4*

"Against them [infidels] make ready your strength to the witness of your power, including seeds of war, to strike terror in the hearts of the enemies of Allah and your enemies" *Sura 8: 60*

"Annihilate the infidels and the polytheists, your [Allah's] enemies and the enemies of the religion. Allah, count them and kill them to the last one" and fight them on until there is no more tumult or oppression, and there prevails justice and faith in Allah altogether and everywhere" *Sura 8: 39*

"Be harsh and ruthless to those who do not believe" *Sura 48: 29*

"Muslims are the best of people" *Sura 3: 110* and unbelievers are "the vilest of created beings" *Sura 98: 6*

These are but a few of the many texts showing that it is Islam itself that commands violence and death to unbelievers so that the whole world be submitted to Islam and to God's holy law of *sharia*. What is so Islamaphobia in pointing out this truth? This is a basic lesson which our leaders in the West either are ignorant of or refuse to accept or believe. Sometimes holdings and opinions are so preposterous that people simply refuse to believe that they can or will be done even when they are written down in black and white. In 1938 when Hitler promised in

*Mein Kamph* that he would kill all the Jews in Europe, people in the West refused to believe it because it seemed so preposterous. Hitler kept his promise by killing six million Jews and untold others in his many death camps.

This *jihad* is there commanded in the *Quran*. This is not Islamaphobia or bashing Islam; it is simply telling the truth from the sacred texts of that religion. Either it is true or it is not true, a Muslim believes it or he must explain it away which he cannot do and remain a faithful Muslim. How does a Muslims explain away a text he is supposed to accept literally? Now you understand why Muslims never want to speak of these texts or try to explain them to us. Those of us who do recite them and ask for an explanation are accused of racism or Islamaphobia. Every time a Muslim suicide bomber blows himself up killing many innocents, we are told that is not Islam. Then what is true Islam? We are never told since the *jihadist* cites the same texts as the peaceful Muslim. Who is correct? We cannot know since there is no central authority to tell us. We have a right to know how they interpret these frightening texts of their own holy books.

The relationship between the house of Islam and the house of war is and can only be war or subjugation. That is the clear teaching of the *Quran*. Why else do you think that Islam divides the world between the two houses? *Dar al-harb* for lands where Islam does not rule equals war; *dar al Islam* where Islam does rule equals peace. There can be no peace according to the *Quran* until the whole world is subject to God's law (*sharia*). That is a basic teaching of Islam. For example, the expression that one who kills an innocent person is as if he killed the whole human race (this is taken from Jewish theology). We are not told that in Islam, the expression only refers to fellow Muslims not to an infidel. Clearly infidels may be killed and should be killed precisely because they are infidels.

This religion is therefore also a political ideology, a religious ideology that seeks to subject the whole world to *sharia* either by non violent Islamization (e.g. as in Europe and in the U.S.) or by war and terror (as in the Middle East and elsewhere). It is a religion that rules every aspect of life via *sharia*. It's as simple as that. This war for submission of the whole world has been going on since the time of Mohammad who led his armies into many battles according to the *Hadith*. Islam has conquered and spread by violent means to, the Near East, Turkey, North Africa, Sudan, parts of Spain, as far east as China and as far south as Indonesia. Islam has been subdued since 1683 when its forward thrust was stopped at Lepanto by Christian armies (the Crusades as defensive wars, failed). This is simply basic history. Are we now to believe that Islam all of a sudden when it has no power, is a peaceful religion having given up *jihad*? This is hardly credible. The twenty first century struggle by the *jihadists* all over the world is only an extension and continuation of that fourteen hundred year war derived from the same sacred books as peaceful Muslims. Both groups have the same objective. This is a global conflict between Islamic civilization and its values and non Islamic civilization and its values; it is Islam versus the rest of the world. That is the nature of the war today - a war of which our leaders are ignorant or volitionally blind. That makes this war global in nature and should be of concern to the whole world not just to the West since its object is global.

This conclusion is so terrible and frightening that the leaders in the West in general and the leaders of the United States in particular refuse to contemplate this much less understand it. So the West uses such bromides as that "Islam is a religion of peace" when all the historical evidence shows just the opposite. Few in number in the West, they are pictured as victims. These leaders try to distinguish peaceful Muslims from violent ones. Yet by what authority do they do this since there is no central authority in Islam to tell us which is true and correct since they both refer and use the same sacred texts. Our leaders have become theologians! Our leaders even try to change the names of this conflict to confuse the rest of us. It is no longer a war on Islamic terrorism but an individual disruption abroad; a *jihadist* is now simply a terrorist or extremist. This is absurd. One who bombs an abortion clinic is an extremist. A *jihadist* is a religious fighter engaged in a holy war to destroy and/or convert the whole world by all means necessary, subversive and otherwise. This means that there will be global peace for Islam only when the whole world is subjected to God's holy law - *sharia*. Until then, there is only a holy war - *jihad* - against unbelievers which is incumbent on all male Muslims. There are peaceful Muslims; there is no peaceful Islam since its very core is one of submission and conquest to establish *sharia* globally. Why are western leaders so blind as not to see this? Islam in their midst is a danger that must be constantly monitored.

This *jihad* may be violent or non violent depending on the situation at hand. It may be *jihad* or a slow Islamization as in the West called 'accommodation.' Terrorism after all is a method to accomplish another goal: the submission to the demands of the terrorist which is common to both groups, violent and non violent Muslims. In a non violent *jihad the object is the same as a violent jihad but by other means*: "accommodation." those who want to expose this fear are intimidated by fear of being named an Islamaphobe, a racist or other such nomenclature. There is also the fear of violence as manifested in the Danish cartoons fiasco, the *Quran* desecration and riots and even threats on the life of Pope Benedict XVI for uttering the truth about Islam, namely, that Islam is a violent religion and that there is no place for violence in religion and that God is a reasonable God not a voluntaristic one. This fear gripped the American media when it refused to publish those Danish cartoons even in a book purporting to explain the Danish phenomenon. The First Amendment was thereby trashed all across this nation. This is the introduction of *sharia* into America even if done non violently by obsequious Americans.

Non violent *jihad* is a slow integration of Islamic values to replace those values contrary to Islam. This is slowly happening in the U.S. where Muslims do not have the power to really change the country by violent means. American Muslims demand more and more accommodation so as to live by their own values and traditions which are diametrically opposed to Judeo-Christian values here in America. Whole areas in America live under Islamic law where many Muslims congregate, e.g. Lackawanna, New York and Dearborn, Michigan. As Lincoln said in 1858, this country cannot live side by side with slavery and freedom. One or the other had to survive but not both. So it is either Islamic values from the *Quran* or American values of equality and religious freedom from the Constitution but not both. The two value systems are absolutely incompatible. By many polls taken, a good number of Muslims living in the West want to live under *sharia* law. They must realize that this is not possible and they must make a choice: *sharia* or American values. If *sharia*, they must not make America their home. So far, our leaders have not made this known clearly to Muslims immigrating to this country.

Our leaders therefore must stop talking about terrorism as if it has no relationship to Islam. "Kill the unbelievers wherever you find them" (*Sura* 9: 5). Is there any other way of understanding this text of the *Quran*? The overwhelming number of places where violence is happening in the world today are committed by Islamic elements following this command and seeking conquest In the words of Ayatollah Khomeini, "The sword is the key to paradise which can be opened only by the holy warriors." We must admit that Khomeini was only following in the footsteps of Mohammad himself in violent *jihad*. And Bin Laden the same. Why deny what is clearly evident? Mohammad's followers want to return to the seventh century because Islam cannot live in a rational modernity ruled by reason and secular law.

The *jihadists* like Bin Laden take Islam seriously in word and in deed. All Muslims would be radicalized if they took Islam and its holy texts seriously and literally. They would join with Bin Laden who rejects reason and modernity which are a threat to Islam. Westerners love life too much and will sacrifice only to the gods of Venus and materialism. Muslims - real Muslims - love death as an opening to heaven for those who fight for Islam (martyrdom). Americans are afraid to die while the latter want to die in honor of their God, Allah, who assures them of heaven. Death for the holy warriors is only a transition to a better place: paradise. That is why they fight so willingly and so ferociously. Since the West has nothing to live for except materialism and consumerism, they are afraid of death as the worst calamity that can befall them because it is a denial of their basic values.

All this cannot be air brushed by bromides such as "Islam is a religion of peace" which is nothing more than Islamic propaganda for Americans by those propagandists who want to cover Islam's reality. It most certainly is not a religion of peace because it has always been a violent religion of conquest of the whole world to subject it to *sharia by the command of Allah himself* in the *Quran,* past and present and by the paradigmatic example of Mohammad, the perfect man. There can be no escaping this basic fact and unless western leaders accept this basic truth about Islam, they are signing their own death warrant and committing suicide by abandoning their values by submission to Islamic values. Both cannot exist side by side. They are contradictory. This is a terrible thing to accept but unless we in the West see Islam for what it really is, in a sense we have *already been defeated. We have only to wait for its final consummation slowly but surely in the triumph of sharia.* Our Christian ancestors fought Islam for hundreds of years to keep it at bay. They were ancestors of faith willing to die for its defense. Having lost its spiritual roots, unlike our ancestors, the West grows weaker by the day because it refuses to fight and die for values that either no longer exist or in which the West no longer believes. You fight and die for values, not for materialism, consumerism and secularism. Who will win such a war? The answer is quite clear. The one who is willing to die in defense of his values is the one who will win. The West is clearly losing this war.

# CHAPTER 6

# "WE ARE AT WAR" SAYS THE PRESIDENT

PRESIDENT OBAMA FINALLY ADMITS that we are at war. The wake up call for everyone was Flight 253 over Detroit that could have resulted in another 9/11. There was a previous murderous episode at Fort Hood, Texas by an Islamic fundamentalist but the real wake up call was Flight 253 because it directly affected the people of the United States. That could have been any one of us or our relatives or friends. That woke up even the President as he finally admitted that "we are at war" with a specific enemy, Al Qaeda. But the enemy is broader than that because these are all different names but the same Islamic fundamentalism with the same goal, i.e. the destruction of our way of life. People must realize that. That being the wake up call, we must put the nation on a war footing to prepare the country accordingly. Here are some pointers vital in war:

   – A selective call up by the draft to fill vital areas needed by the military. All young men and women ages 19-26 to be put on notice of a call up at any time so as to minimize any disruption in their lives. They must be prepared to serve if called. This is war.

   – A surcharge on all taxes, income, corporate and excise is needed to pay for the war. All citizens must realize that all must sacrifice in some way to pay for the war and not leave it to future generations. This is called common sacrifice in a war effort.

   – There must be a declaration of war by Congress to give the President all constitutional power to conduct war here and abroad. That declaration is against Islamic fundamentalists by whatever name they go by. Without such a declaration, there are genuine constitutional obstacles for conduct by the President, domestically and internationally. This war power should include such things as surveillance, wire tapping, draft call up, etc. These actions will then be legal and appropriate in the extraordinary circumstances of war until the war is won.

   – An educational thrust is required to prepare the nation about the nature of this war, about our enemy, who he is, what he believes and why we fight him in the first place. In a democracy, the people must know whom they fight and why they fight because it is the people who are called on to bear the burden of war. In a time of war, all can be called upon to serve, thus suspending the volunteer army for the length of the war. We must identify the enemy as Islamic fundamentalists or *jihadists* and no longer be politically correct by avoiding the name and reality of this species of religious extremism of Islam.

– Special surveillance of mosques, preachings of imams, what Islamic schools teach, etc. Since *jihadists* get the impetus and inspiration from the texts of Islam, all this special surveillance is legitimate in time of war since we cannot tell the difference between moderate Muslims and *jihadists*. We must carefully distinguish moderate Muslims from *jihadists*. In this, Muslims themselves must help by reporting the violent ones in their midst. It was wrong to incarcerate those of Japanese ancestry during WWII because they were Japanese. But it was not wrong for all those of Japanese ancestry to be specially screened for the nation's survival. The same with Muslims in America since our enemy derives his inspiration from this religion, rightly or wrongly. The Muslim community in America has a special obligation to explain Islam to us and how it really is a "religion of peace." This will be a difficult task given the many passages of war and hatred of infidels in the *Quran*. If American Muslims refuse to denounce the *jihadists* in their communities, they all fall under suspicion.

– A declaration of war will clear up once and for all that all those caught here or abroad conducting war, subversion and terrorism against the United States, are combatants. They will be treated as prisoners of war under the Geneva Protocols and not be treated as common criminals to be tried in civilian courts. They will be tried by military tribunals with all the rights of POWs. American citizens so caught will be tried for treason in the United States by United States courts with the full rights of American citizens.

– We must prepare the citizenry about fear of terrorism here at home and how to live with that fear as we did in WWII (e.g. blackouts, discussion groups, neighbor watching out for neighbor, etc.). If we are at war, there is a natural fear domestically but we must learn to live with it in the name of the values we fight for. We fight for our survival and for the survival of our way of life against those who desire to destroy it and substitute a universal caliphate under Islam with its own values which contradict our values. That is the core reason we are attacked and why we fight.

Either the war affects all of us or we are only fooling ourselves. War involves all Americans. Patriotism and our survival demands nothing less in a time of war.

# CHAPTER 7

# HOW TO LIVE WITH ISLAM

ISLAM IS AT A crossroads. The global non Muslim community almost everywhere is at war with radical or fundamentalist or *jihadist* Islam: Nigeria, Philippines, Thailand, Indonesia, Iraq, Iran, Afghanistan, Pakistan, India, America, England, Spain, France, Chechnya, etc. It seems that the *jihadists* are active all over the world following in the footsteps of Mohammad and his proclamation of violent *jihad* against the infidel. To a degree Islam has historically succeeded by violent conquest until the end of the seventeenth century when the Ottomans were defeated and turned back in 1683. The final blow was WWI and the break up of the Ottoman Empire. Muslims have been powerless ever since. Bin Laden has attempted to stir up *jihadists* and he has succeeded to a degree.

But it should be clear that not only is the West and the United States no match militarily for the *jihadists*; in addition, the non Islamic world is unwilling to submit to violent Islam and they will fight if necessary. The *jihadists* can do a lot of damage by terrorism almost everywhere and at will, but they will not succeed in establishing a caliphate neither in Islamic countries nor certainly in the West.

The value system of Islam - *sharia* - and the democracy of the West are absolutely incompatible and the *jihadists* will not succeed in destroying the freedom of the West purchased with so much effort and blood. Americans will fight if they are pushed hard enough. Because they are ignorant of the contrary value system of Islam and *sharia*, Americans want to "get along" and live in peace with Muslims. This good will of course is not shared by the *jihadists* but the problem is that we cannot distinguish between violent *jihadists* and those Muslims who want to live in peace. More ominously, peaceful Muslims are unwilling to give up the violent ones in their midst so that every time a *jihadist* blows himself up, killing many innocents, the only response we get from Muslims is that "that is not Islam." They never seem to tell us what real Islam is except the cliche that it is a "religion of peace." Then where do the *jihadists* learn their violence and hatred since they read the same holy books as those who want to live in peace - the *Quran*, the *Hadith*, the *Sira*? A serious reading of these holy books evinces a lot of hatred for Jews and infidels and many calls to war on and killing of non Muslims all of whom (unless they become Muslim) are going to hell. This is a question that is never addressed by Americans to Muslims nor answered by Muslims except by cliches. A close investigation of these holy books clearly shows that the values contained in them are absolutely incompatible with American values contained in our founding documents of the Declaration of Independence and our

Constitution (e.g. religious freedom for all, universal equality, human rights inherent in each person, separation of church and state, democracy, free speech to criticize any religion, secular law separated from theology, etc.). Each and every one of these American values is in direct contradiction with the holy *sharia* law of Islam. This conclusion may be distasteful for many Americans who "just want to get along" but you cannot have two contradictory sets of values living side by side in the same country. Either one will prevail and the other lose or visa-versa. Examine the two and then tell me how the two can possibly live side by side.

It was the same conundrum faced by Lincoln in 1858: we can't live in the same country half free and half slave. They are contradictory and we face the same situation in this country when we say that we want to live in peace with Islam. That is not possible and the sooner Americans realize this, the safer they will be. A Muslim who seriously reads the holy books of Islam and takes its teachings literally, must become a *jihadist* or leave aside much of the teaching of the *Quran*. For example, how can you believe in religious freedom for all and still hold with the *Quran* (the very word of God come down from heaven) that anyone who leaves Islam for another religion, should be put to death? Since the *Quran* must be read literally, there is no getting around this holding and that of American religious freedom which holds that in conscience anyone can leave or join any religion he or she wishes. Or have none at all. It is easy to see this contradiction so that one must choose one set of values or the other. There is no *via media*.

Moderate Muslims may hold to their teaching (e.g. death to Jews, Christians, infidels) as something that will happen only at the end of time, in God's time and place. If these teachings of the holy books were allegorized this way, i.e. happening only at the end, all of us non Muslims could live side by side with Muslims, knowing that at any time they would not turn on us as many American Muslims already have (e.g. Fort Hood massacre). Muslims could then try to convert anyone they wish as long as it is done freely and non violently. That is the nature of religious freedom. Many Christians have become Muslims in this country without a whiff of threats, intolerance or violence.

That is the choice today for Muslims in the West and in particular, those in the United States. They must not try to introduce Islamic values by a slow accommodation called Islamization which is a stealth form of non violent *jihad*. If Muslims come to this country, they must live by American values and not try to make Americans bow to Muslim values which are incompatible with American values. If Muslims want to live by *sharia*, they should not make America their home and they should find a country where that holy law is observed and obeyed. And that country is not America.

This is a hard saying but there is no other way to say it and remain a loyal American observing the values of freedom handed down to us from our forefathers and for which so many gave their "last full measure of devotion." This must never be surrendered to a value system that is completely opposed to American values. That is pure treason. Muslims must not come to this country thinking that they can convert us to alien values. If they come here, they must live by our American values or they should not come here at all.

That is the crossroads for Muslims in America. Americans are beginning to realize this little by little in recent polls which show that almost two thirds of Americans today either distrust Islam or are strongly opposed to Islam. You cannot have Muslim Americans all over the country betraying and killing their fellow Americans without the rest of America waking up as to the true nature and holding of this religion. The time has come for us non Muslims to be honest and forthright with Muslim Americans living in this country and abroad as well. Uncomfortable as that might be.

How to live with Islam? Literally according to the *Quran*, not possible. Allegorized to the end of time, quite possible. Which one to pursue is for Muslims to decide.

# CHAPTER 8

# PREREQUISITES FOR ANY DIALOGUE BETWEEN MUSLIMS AND OTHER AMERICANS

IT WAS THOMAS FRIEDMAN who asked the crucial question about Islam: when a suicide bomber blows himself up along with dozens of innocents, Muslims tell us that is not Islam. But then they never tell us what Islam is. More to the point, there is seldom any massive protest by American Muslims against these acts of violence by their fellow Muslims. Condemnations are even far fewer.

We Americans really want to believe our fellow American Muslims who in fact mostly do live in peace and want to be loyal Americans in their respect for religious freedom and for the pluralism of American culture. Some of us, however, have serious doubts about this when we see case after case of home grown American Muslims who have been caught red handed committing acts of terror or conspiracy to commit terror on their fellow Americans. For example, there are now five American Muslims in Pakistan jails who openly admit to going to Afghanistan to kill American soldiers. We also think of the massacre of Fort Hood by an American major in the name of Islam. Is their allegiance to Islam and fellow Muslims greater than their allegiance to the United States? We need an honest dialogue with Muslims in this country about Islam for some answers to these questions. We can no longer be politically correct by not asking and answering these questions.

The most recent attacks on American citizens came from a Nigerian Muslim. On Christmas day, 2009, Abdul Mudallah, a Nigerian national tried to detonate an incendiary device as the Northwest Airline 330 was attempting to land in Detroit with 279 passengers on board. He wanted to be a suicide bomber by taking all these innocent Americans along with him. Fortunately the device failed to completely detonate and all passengers survived. Yet there has not been one protest from the American Muslim community, not one march for an event which is much more serious than any cartoon depicting Mohammad as a bomb thrower. When there are no marches or massive protests against these horrendous acts by American Muslims, we non Muslim Americans have every right to be suspicious of anything Islamic/Muslim no matter how many protests of loyalty are forthcoming from the Muslim community in America. We need an honest dialogue about the relationship between Islam and these iniquitous acts of violence. Is there an inherent relationship? Suspicions are growing. Unless such a dialogue is forthcoming between the Muslim community and other Americans, suspicion of Muslims and Islam will continue to grow with every anti American act by American Muslims in America. The example of Hassan and his massacre of fellow soldiers at Fort Hood, Texas now demands such a dialogue. Clearly if this does not happen, Americans will more and more demand that immigration of Muslims into this country be curtailed and a more stringent investigation and surveillance of Muslims, their mosques and schools in this country be conducted as a dangerous and suspect group.

The prerequisites to any such dialogue I believe to be four in number. Without agreement on all four of these basic prerequisites, any dialogue with Muslims in this country (or abroad) becomes virtually impossible. In fact, without their agreement, there can only be a growing suspicion of the whole Muslim enterprise in this country and around the world. It is now time for honest dialogue.

1. There must be a true and unequivocal condemnation of suicide bombers or better, of homicidal suicidals. The killing of innocents who are unarmed and peaceful is a moral perversion and we must hear that loud and clear from the Muslim community in this country. So far only sporadic condemnations have been heard from American Muslims but no massive condemnation, marches or protest against this abomination. Until we do, our suspicions will only grow of the whole Muslim enterprise in this country. There are imams and Islamic spokespersons around the world who in fact hold that such attacks are in full agreement with the *Quran* and *Hadith* as a legitimate form of self defense against the enemies of Islam. In the words of Arie Kruglanski, a professor of psychology at the University of Maryland who studied videotapes of suicide bombers' final words and interviews with the mothers, says that the overwhelming motivation of suicide bombers is the quest for personal meaning and a desperate longing for a meaningful life that appears only tome with death. This is completely unacceptable to Americans and must be loudly and vociferously condemned by the Islamic community in America and elsewhere for there to be any reasonable dialogue.

2. The virulent anti Semitism and anti Jewish hatred and rejection must stop. This anti Semitism is deeply ingrained in various places in the *Quran* and I do not know how Muslims can overcome such virulent hatred and rejection. I only know that any dialogue between Muslims in America and other Americans will go nowhere unless Muslims give up this preaching-teaching-holding of Jewish hatred. This is simply to single out an innocent group of Americans for hatred because they are Jewish which is unacceptable to Americans. Some progress has been made in this regard but it needs a firm commitment from the Islamic community that this is not part of its agenda. Criticism of Israel is perfectly legitimate. What is not legitimate is advocacy of Israel's annihilation and destruction. We are too far along in history for any such a form of genocide to be acceptable.

3. The right to religious freedom everywhere is another prerequisite to any Muslim-American dialogue. In this country, Muslims have every right to build and worship in mosques, establish their own schools and the creation of subsidiary groups pushing for Islamic understanding and interests as well as to proselytize those who would freely enter into Islam. This unfortunately is not the case in too many Islamic countries. Muslims attack Copts in Egypt; Chaldean Christians are murdered and their churches are bombed in Iraq; Christians are jailed in Pakistan for any criticism of Islam under its blasphemy laws; there is open warfare on Christians in Sudan and Nigeria to enforce Islam on them - and much more. In fact, in

the *Quran* itself, there is decreed death for anyone who leaves Islam. Whatever this means, this is most emphatically not religious freedom and must be rejected out of hand. It is either religious freedom for all as an inherent human right or any dialogue with Islam becomes extremely difficult if not impossible. Religious freedom must always be a two way street where one is inherently free to enter or exit any religion as the conscience of the individual dictates. It is not one thing when Muslims are a minority and harassment/attack when Muslims are a majority. Religious freedom is an inherent human right for all and not just for Muslims. This pre-requisite of religious freedom for all as an inherent human right is non negotiable for dialogue between Muslims and non Muslims. If not, any dialogue between Muslims and other non Muslims becomes virtually impossible.

4. The fourth prerequisite is one of respect for the good faith of all other non Muslim religions and even atheism. This is really a respect for conscience which is the voice of God in each person. Even when we consider the other to be following an erroneous path religiously or even morally (unless it affects the common good), we must respect the conscience of all in any true dialogue between Muslims and non Muslims. This has not always been the case on both sides. I may think that my faith encompasses the unique and even total truth about God, society, my fellow men, etc. But I must still respect the conscience of the one who believes differently for whatever reason. I must presuppose that the other speaks the truth to me as he sees it and I to him. He must be truthful even if his views are erroneous. Otherwise no dialogue is possible.

These four principles are prerequisites to any true dialogue between Muslims/non Muslims not only in America but all over the whole world. All must agree on all four pre requisites in their totality (not just one or two or three) or any fruitful dialogue between the two groups becomes all but impossible. Why so? Because these are moral-ethical conditions that go to the heart of human behavior. They are not political conditions, e.g. the existence or non existence of the state of Israel. In fact, they relate to our nature as humans which cannot be compromised or attenuated. There must be no more politically correct attempts to avoid this basic ethical condition of our common nature. Any dialogue between Christians and Islam is all but impossible for both sides.

# CHAPTER 9

# SOME ELEMENTS OF
# DIALOGUE WITH ISLAM

RECENT DEBATES ON ISLAM as Islamic integral or jihadist Islam has caused great confusion among the American people: how to distinguish between peaceful Muslims and violent ones. The American people are becoming more and suspicious of Islam and Muslims especially since in the last year alone, there have been many attempts by Muslim operatives (and they alone) to bring mayhem to these shores (e.g. a Somali Muslim who tried to blow up an airplane over Detroit, the Islamic major who murdered thirteen at Fort Hood, and the most recent case of a native American Muslim who tried to ignite a car bomb in Times Square in New York City). Some basic questions must be asked if we are to have a reasonable dialogue with American Muslims in the United States and not repeat the mantra of "Islam is a religion of peace" when sections of it are not. Here are some questions and answers which will give us only a partial view.

*Can we live with Islam?* There is first the problem of all the question of integration of Muslims into the values of America. This seems to be difficult for some Muslim immigrants who come from countries that are completely Islamic and who have lived under the Muslim law of *sharia*. In Islam there is no real separation of church and state. But other Muslims vary in this. They all call themselves Muslims but differently. It is a question of how will we live with Muslims in an America whose basic values are different from those in the *Quran* and its holy law, *sharia*. We should remember that the relation between Islam and Christianity goes back some fourteen hundred years and those years have been ones mostly of confrontation, conflict and open warfare as Muslim armies swept across North Africa and as far as Spain and Vienna. Christians had to fight a defensive war for survival.

*What has changed in this relationship in the past fifty years or so in historical perspective?* The causes are evident and concrete. First of all there is the demographic problem. Islamic countries have not experienced (as in Europe and the United States) the demographic suicide (In Europe there are only 1.3 children per European woman. Muslims have much larger families.) These Islamic countries also have economic problems where technology and industrialization (modernization) have not progressed. There is oil rich Saudi Arabia which favors and finances a rigorous (and violent) Islam which proselytizes all over the world. Today's Islam has not modernized economically precisely because these Islamic countries are not free because of their religion. There is a struggle between those Muslims who want to return to the original Islam of the seventh century and who those desire modernization. There are also historical problems of colonization by the West which have left bitter memories of oppression and humiliation. We must add the internal corruption and autocratic leaders of many Islamic nations which is largely tolerated. This gives rise to the fundamentalists who say that Islam is the answer. All this gives way to a sentiment of revenge for which Christians in the East are today the victims. Most Arabs in America are Christians fleeing intolerance of Arab Muslims who want to purify their countries from Christians who are looked upon as foreign oppressors.

*For a dialogue there must be two partners. Is Islam ready for dialogue and is there something inherent in Islam that cannot change?* We Christians are part of the dialogue and I am not sure whether it is "we" who are ready to dialogue. There are profound prejudices on both sides. Then there is the word 'ready' which can mean prepared by knowledge of each other and disposition toward each other (knowledge and will). Then what kind of a dialogue are we speaking? What shall we discuss? On economics, international politics and urbanization, we can speak with Muslims to iron out differences and compromises the best we can.

At the religious level the dialogue is extremely difficult. Islam has defined for itself to distinguish itself from Christianity and the Bible. Islam has given the Bible an interpretation and defined central personages in an original and different way, to distinguish themselves from Christians and Jews. Muslims often think they know about Christianity and Judaism which they consider to be something now bypassed by Islam as their ultimate perfection. Christianity for Muslims is old history and perhaps falsified history. Most Christians have the advantage that they do not know Islam. Yet, too many Christians think that the Abraham of Jesus and of Islam are the same as Christian understanding. This is profoundly false. The two interpretations could not be more divergent in interpretation.

*Can we speak of Islam in general? Are there not really many Islams which differ in ways of living and defining the Islamic faith?* There is much truth in this statement. The traditional subjected people under Islam, are very different. The practice of Egyptians or Mauritanians do not coincide. There are different nations, judicial schools, different confraternities which can hate each other or even fight each other - without even mentioning the differences between Shiites and Sunnis. This said, it is Muslims themselves who speak of Islam in general. They all feel as one in the "home of Islam" and all read the same *Quran* as dictated by God to Mohammad; all have Mecca for their pilgrimage - *haj* - to be done once in a lifetime for each Muslim and all pray five times a day in the direction of Mecca, the holiest of cities.

Clearly, integral Islam (or fundamentalist Islam) is not all of Islam. But these jihadists or fundamentalists do refer to the *Quran* and justify what they do in the name of the *Quran* and the teaching of Mohammad. By what authority can they be said not to be legitimate? There is no central authority in Islam like there is for the Pope of Catholicism. By what right do some Americans - including the President of the United States - speak of "true" Islam as opposed to the "false" Islam that uses terrorism as their weapon? How can any of them say that violent jihadists are a corruption of "true Islam"? That is impossible and the fundamentalists are as Islamic as any others. That's the real problem! Western leaders console themselves by distinguishing "true" Islam from "false" Islam.

*What is the true nature of Islam as a religion?* To make distinctions shows that westerners apply their categories to Islam which are really western categories. Our concept of "religion" is really drawn from Christianity such as separation of church and state. Islam understands itself as a way of total living which includes the totality of life: the relation to God as well as the total daily life of the individual which includes food, dress, family, knowledge, marriage, etc.. Society is governed by the one law of *sharia* which rules them all. In other words, Islam is a total religion where there is no separation of church and state or any form of "privacy" in religion or secular matters. One leaves Islam under penalty of death (apostasy) because one thereby leaves the truth.

*What of the wearing of the burqa over the total face of a woman which is outlawed in many countries in Europe and even in America over such issues as drivers licenses?* This question is serious for Europeans. It is outlawed in France and Belgium as are the minarets in Switzerland. All this is not contained in the *Quran* but these practices are symbolic. The *Quran* commands women to cover themselves and the burqa is a particular application of that command which is particularly strict. For Islam, however, the unique legislator is God and his holy law must be followed irrespective of any secular law. This applies even in matters of dress and food. Conflict in this area when Muslims move to the West is inevitable. Muslims in countries like England and Canada desire to be ruled by Islamic religious law (*sharia*) and not by secular law.

*What is the result of all this in a secular society like the United States where the separation of church and state is a basic and secular American value?* The real origin of the secular state started in France and the French Revolution in opposition to the Catholic Church. The strict separation of church and state was taken up by the original authors of the United States Constitution who had suffered as well from religious intolerance from which many of them fled. They separated religion from the political as a solution to religious intolerance. This poses a real problem for Muslims in America. Islam considers itself one nation (*umma*) which transcends national boundaries between peoples. Islam considers nationalism a dangerous form of idolatry. Its vocation is global which poses difficulties for Muslims worldwide in separate nations. The allegiance of many Muslims is to the *umma* not to nation states.

*We must protect against religious assimilation but must we separate the understanding of the God of Christianity from other views of God?* Of course we must. It is of great interest to understand other religions to be able to better dialogue with them. We must know the differences which makes them different. We must not deny who we are which would be the end of real dialogue. We must guard ourselves against sentimentalism that we all believe in one God or that we are all headed in the same direction. Christians and Muslims both believe in a unique God but not in the same way which is unique in both the Bible and in Islam. We recognize the same biblical personages but our history and meaning of them is radically different. We both believe in a last judgment but the mercy of God produces different effects according to Christianity and Islam. What really makes us similar is our common humanity: reason and the virtues. On this plane there can be mutual respect and reciprocal admiration. For example, we insist on saying that we both adhere to and believe in one God. But which? How do we know which God is good? How to identify the true God and distinguish him from concurring Gods? *We have one criterium: the true God demands nothing because he only gives. A false God - on the contrary - makes demands.* That finally is the radical difference between Christianity and Islam.

# CHAPTER 10

# CAN WE REALLY DIALOGUE WITH ISLAM?

IT IS DIFFICULT TO understand the view of the Obama administration, namely, that he wants to speak with our enemies without any preconditions. It is strange because our enemies -Bin Laden, Iran, Hezbollah, The Muslim Brotherhood, Hamas, Al Qaeda and their Islamic allies - have told him and all of us to our face that they want to destroy our way of life and kill us all in the name of Islam. Even if they are a minority, that still represents millions of people. They make no bones about it and they justify this position as a struggle against the great Satan. They are mandated to conduct this war (*jihad*) by their holy books, the *Quran* and the *Hadith*, and by the example of their prophet Mohammad who himself mandated *jihad* against all infidels who are simply filth and destined for hell. Is it because President Obama in spite of his Islamic upbringing as a young child does not know the content of the *Quran* and the example of Mohammad who is paradigmatic for all Muslims? That is hard to believe because he has educated Muslims on his advisory staff.

If one understands our enemies and their holy books and the example of Mohammad that they are sworn to follow and obey as the very will of God, how do you change them unless you change the very texts that mandate the destruction, killing and conquering of all infidels? There is the core question which so many Americans do not want to face. That simply is not possible unless you are ignorant of the content of those holy writings and the very example of Mohammad who led his armies into seventy two battles of conquest. Our enemies keep on telling us that this is the religious foundation of this war as well as of their attitude against us and everything we stand for. They justify this war therefore by divine mandate. They think that they cannot lose this war because Allah is on their side. It is for our enemies, a religious war - *jihad* - which mandates struggle to the death - theirs or ours.

If I may, let me quote few chapters from these holy books which will lift the veil from what our enemies believe and plan to do: "I will instill terror into the hearts of the unbelievers: smite ye above their necks and smite all the fingertips of them" (*Quran* 8:12). Allah is not satisfied with killing unbelievers but must torture them as well before killing them.

The *Quran* tells Muslims to kill unbelievers wherever they find them (2: 191), murder them and treat them harshly (9: 123), fight them (8:65) until no other religion other than Islam is left (2: 193). Muslims must humiliate unbelievers and impose on them a penalty tax if they are Christians or Jews (9;29), slay them if they are pagans (9:5); crucify or cut off their hands and feet and expel them from the land in disgrace. Muslims are told that unbelievers "shall have a great punishment in the world hereafter" (5:34) and not to befriend their own fathers and brothers if they are not believers (3:28; 9:23), kill their own family as in the battle of Badr and Ohud and "to strive against the unbeliever with great endeavor" (25:52). Muslims must be stern with unbelievers because they belong in hell (66:9). "Strike off the heads of unbelievers" then after a "wide slaughter among them, carefully tie up the remaining captives" (47: 4). The *Quran* denies freedom of belief for all and clearly states that Islam is the only acceptable religion (3: 85). Allah relegates those who do not believe in the *Quran* to hell (5: 11) and calls them *najis* - filthy, untouchable, impure (9: 28). Unbelievers will go to hell and drink boiling water (14: 17). Husbands have a right to beat their wives (4: 34) and women will go to hell if they are disobedient to their husbands (66: 10). The *Quran* not only denies women equal rights to inheritance (4: 11-12), it also regards them as imbeciles and decrees that their testimony alone is not admissible in court (2: 282). A woman who is raped cannot accuse her rapist unless she can produce four male witnesses. Allah allows Muslims to rape women captured in wars even if They are married before capture (4: 3, 24). According to *sharia* (holy law) the government is not allowed to kill a father if he kills his daughter or son for any reason. All *kafirs* (unbelievers) go to hell. A Muslim can be a killer and murder non Muslims and yet be a righteous person and not be held accountable. Any Muslim who leaves the faith must be put to death.

These are only a few of the holdings and tenets of the holy books of Islam. How does a non believer like Obama even as president hope "to talk" with these people in the Muslims world - or any where else - who believe such things and who are bound to follow these texts and tenets *as the very word of God*? That is very difficult to believe and only a fool who is interested in self death would attempt to do so. These tenets and beliefs are not made up smears from an Islamaphobe but are contained in the very writings of a text supposed to be the very words of God dictated (*Quran*) to Mohammad and cannot be understood except in a literal sense. It is Bin Laden and Al Qaeda that have correctly interpreted the *Quran* and not so called "moderates" who dare not explain them. Before Obama as president sits down to talk "unconditionally" with people of such beliefs, he should read this "holy" book and be acquainted with what his enemy holds *vis-a-vis* him and the people he represents in America because they are in fact infidels according to the *Quran*. Given this teaching (and I have cited only a few of these texts and holdings) which are sacred and unrepealable by our enemies, how does Obama purport "to talk" with them with no preconditions? All this should lead us to a frightening conclusion: it is not a part of Islam that is opposed to us infidels *but perhaps Islam itself as revealed by the very sacred books of Islam that want to kill us as unbelievers.* Last but not least, a Muslim in the interest and promotion of Islam, may lie to an infidel like Obama, president or not. How will Obama ever be sure that when his enemies speak that they are telling him the truth? He cannot. Like Jimmy Carter, who talked with the leaders of Hezbollah and claimed that they are willing to recognize Israel. That very afternoon, it was categorically denied by that same leader. Our enemies therefore will say one thing and do another. Western ethics forbids lies while Islam may promote lies in the interest and promotion of Islam. There will be peace but only when the whole world is converted to Islam by any means necessary, peaceful or violent. That is the meaning of peace in the *Quran*.

If Obama understands any of this, namely, that Islam is not a "religion of peace," how will he negotiate with our enemies "unconditionally"? Does he not understand what Islam really is? What it intends for us unbelievers? Then he must read Islam's holy books and find out for himself.

Finally, I urge all Americans and all those who want "to talk" with our Islamic enemy to read the *Quran* and simply think about where this religion comes from. Only after understanding what our Islamic enemy believes and holds as the very word of God, can we conclude whether to talk with him or simply conclude that he is a danger to ourselves and all we hold dear in the West and be prepared to fight for our values. Islam is a problem for the whole world and the rest of the world is likely to meet its end as soon as true Muslims assemble the weaponry required to destroy the earth. That is why Iran must never be allowed to have nuclear weapons and the United States and Israel must forbid it by whatever means necessary for our own safety. Even if it means military action. There is no deterrent from the mullahs of Iran because it comes from Shiite religious belief.

Hillaire Belloc, the famous French writer of the last century, believed that Islam would one day pose an even greater danger than that of Hitler's regime. He was acutely aware that historically, "Vienna, as we saw, was almost taken and only saved by the Christian army under the command of the king of Poland [Jan Sobieski] on a date that ought to be the most famous in history - September 11, 1683." In Muslim traditions there is the declaration from the very beginning that the day of resurrection cannot come until faithful Muslims carry out a final holocaust against the Jewish people. A holocaust mandated by the *Quran* itself. How to dialogue with such a religion? *That was before the establishment of the state of Israel.* This mandate for a holocaust is as old as Islam itself. We today are facing the greatest war machine in the history of the world: an ideology that holds that the killing of others, that is, unbelievers, the plundering of their wealth, the conquering of their lands, the enslavement of their people and the destruction of their institutions to be among the highest virtues and stepping stones to salvation. How in God's name do you negotiate with people who really believe that? Nowhere in America is such a question ever asked. It must be asked if we are to survive

What we need in abundance is sacrifice and strength to defend the freedoms of the West. The greatest strength of Islam is the denuded spirituality of the West, a forgetfulness and corruption of its Judeo-Christian roots. Today everything that once made the West great (Judeo-Christian values) and distinguished it from other civilizations has been de-legitimated by decades of relativist battering. We no longer have true believers willing to fight and die for this tradition of freedom. Islam has its true believers who cannot be "talked to," and are willing to die for the spread of Islam everywhere For our enemy, negotiations are a defeat and humiliation. Their central goal is the conversion of all the earth to Islam ("submission") to be ruled by God's sacred law of *sharia*. For Americans and Obama to sit down "to talk" with such people is not only futile, it is an act of national suicide. The real question in the face of such an enemy is: are we willing to sacrifice, fight and die for the preservation of our values, for freedom and for our way of life? Our enemy is prepared to die for his vision and values from the *Quran* as saw on 9/11. Are we ready to do the same? Not to understand the nature of Islam as the driving force of our enemy is to invite our own death and destruction. Obama and his fellow Americans do not seem to understand this simple but basic proposition.

# CHAPTER 11

# SOME SERIOUS DIFFICULTIES IN A DIALOGUE WITH ISLAM

IN AN AGE OF dialogue and understanding, there is one great lacuna: a rational dialogue between Christianity and Islam. And of course, we immediately see the core of the problem: rationality or reason which has been present in Christianity from the beginning but is absent from Islam because of its teaching since the ninth century on God's transcendence.

Pope Benedict XVI has been trying to emphasize the point that there can and should be no violence in matters religious. Yet everywhere in the world there is conflict between the two religions, almost exclusively from the Islamic side: Algeria, Pakistan, Egypt, Lebanon, Indonesia, Bangladesh, the Occupied Territories, Nigeria, Iraq, Iran, Bali, the Philippines - almost every Islamic country is at war with Christianity Violence is always the inability to rationally solve problems which are resolved by force. In matters religious this is really contradictory since God forces no one to believe. But this is true only when we speak in the area of reason. That is the real problem in dialogue here. Thus the first difficulty in the dialogue is reason.

In Islam, the *Quran* is the very word of God which is eternal in nature and was dictated to Mohammad by the Angel Gabriel. If that is so, there can be no other source of truth than the sayings of the *Quran* that contains all truth. Everything is determined by God and man has no freedom except to accept, submit and obey *sharia* - the codification of the *Quran*. All other sources of truth such as *reason* are *eo ipso* excluded and rejected in Islam. The elementary principle of cause/effect is rejected by Islam and is replaced by the direct action of God as a direct causality in all things. The apple falls from the tree not by gravity but by the will of God. Since God's transcendence is causality in all things, all things are already determined by the divine will. Reason and human will have nothing to do with it. The result is that man's will is not really free but determined before hand to which man has only to submit: *Inshallah*, if God wills it, is present in every work of man because it is done by the will of God never by the will of man or by reason,

It is important to remember that human rights as universal principles do not find their root in Islam, only in Judeo-Christianity. Since there is no ontology in Islam of the human person ("created in the image and likeness of God") it is impossible for man to be like God because of God's transcendence. God is bound by nothing, not even his own word. Therefore only Muslims who accept the word of God in *sharia* have human dignity while all others do not. In fact others have no dignity until they accept the word of God's *sharia* and convert to Islam. They are infidels (i.e. filth). Until that happens there are no universal human rights which, once again, is extremely detrimental for any dialogue with the Christian faith and with the United Nations Universal Declaration of Human Rights. It is difficult to really progress in ecumenism when Islam holds such a view of universal human rights *which do not exist in Islam*. Only a Muslim has rights because he obeys God's word which created him. Creation is *ex nihilo* for worship and has nothing to do with reference to God's nature which is absolutely transcendent, beyond all reason, knowledge or relationship. This is in utter contrast to Judeo-Christian ontology where man is in relationship with God in whose image and likeness man is created. Therefore reason has a central place in that relationship because an intelligent God creates intelligently.

This makes it almost impossible to have a true dialogue (or even a development of science for that matter which is essentially related to cause and effect) because there is nothing really to discuss except to accept the total truth contained in the *Quran*. That is why for centuries nothing creative, no inventions, no philosophy, no economic progress was possible in Islam because of a lack of reason: here is the only truth in the *Quran*, accept or reject it with consequences of ignorance in this life and hell fire in the next.

This problem in Islam goes back to the tenth-eleventh century when the great dispute arose about whether the *Quran* is eternal or created. If eternal, then all the above comes about. If the *Quran* is created, it must have been created by a rational God who is both rational and has free will which he bestowed on man. Man is created with freedom, free will and with reason. Therefore man is free to understand God, the universe, himself and to determine his own destiny by his reason. He can find by reason a rational ethical system. This was flat out rejected by the traditionists in Islam who said this was blasphemy because it limited the transcendence and omnipotence of God. The *Quran* is eternal and possesses all truth and cannot be added to. Therefore reason as an independent source of knowledge and action was rejected once and for all since God's causality acts directly on all things. The brilliant age of science, philosophy, medicine and thinking was over having been defeated once and for all by the traditionalists who rejected reason in favor of God's complete transcendence. Man is not free because he was created only to worship God in obedience to God's law of *sharia* and all other sources of knowledge are false and blasphemous as a denial of God's transcendence. That is why Islam has made no progress philosophically, economically, politically, socially, etc, in over a thousand years.

What we now have today is a clash of civilizations where western science and rationality meet the determinism and exclusive truth contained only in the *Quran*. Those Muslims who have moved to and live in the West are torn between the two civilizations and where they practice a religion that is incompatible with western ideals of individual freedom and rationality. That is also the cause of Islam's terrorism and force which is central to the teachings of Bin Laden: modernity, i.e. western thought, he taught, must be rejected and a return to the living exemplar of the original Islamic community of the seventh century. Modernity and reason will destroy Islam. This really is a clash of civilizations which is mortal in nature because they cannot coexist with each other.

It is this inability of western leaders to understand this simple proposition when they think that they can live in peace with Islamic teachings. However there is a core contradiction between the two. They cannot coexist. Either the West converts to Islam - into lands of peace - or there is perpetual conflict between the two - lands of war. Terrorism will exist as long as there is a division between these two essential civilizations. *They cannot coexist and there can be only war.*

This idea of Islam is very difficult if not impossible to be accepted by Christianity and by western culture built on a Judeo-Christian ethic of freedom and reason. From the beginning, Christianity was open to reason and used reason to explicate, explain, develop and understand its own teaching as its handmaid. Of course there are severe limits on reason since faith is transcendent and beyond all reason. But reason is vital because God is a rational being (even if he is more than this) who created rationally. That is why science could develop in the West because reason reflected on cause/effect of the material universe. The universe's laws are rational because creation was rationally created by a knowing and rational God. This is combined with mans' freedom - because he was created in the image and likeness of God who is a rational reality. Man's own destiny is in his hands in freedom as a created creator. Man then can understand himself, the universe and others because he is both rational and free to determine his own destiny. The absence of this in Islam explains why there has been no progress in Islam in a thousand years.

The western view of freedom, rationality and human rights draws its roots and meaning from Judeo-Christianity which both welcomed reason, science, a rational God and man created in his image. Western civilization has produced the greatest freedom and prosperity of western civilization. Judeo-Christianity took matter and its creation by a rational God seriously. This also lays the foundation for universal human rights of all men of all nations who are all created in the image and likeness of God.

Hence the dialogue with Islam is very difficult if not impossible. Indeed as long as Islam's views on *reason*, freedom and human rights remain as we have explained them, it is really impossible. The clash of civilizations - Islamic and western - is real and on going. Sadly, there really can be no compatibility between the two and those Muslims who live in the West suffer schizophrenia of a religion which is incompatible with the values they live under.

# CHAPTER 12

# MY AMERICAN MANIFESTO

THIS IS MY AMERICAN Manifesto in which are contained the values I believe in as an American and as a Christian I expect nothing less from anyone who calls himself an American. What I am speaking about is values, not culture. There are many things in the culture that I despise and object to, e.g. abortion on demand, the homosexual agenda. But no true American can reject the following values and still call himself-herself an American: equality of all persons before the secular law; the equality of the sexes; separation of church and state whose criteria for legislation are reason and history - never theology; religious freedom for every person to adhere to religion or to no religion which he or she believes to be correct without any kind of force, violence or coercion from government or other religious groups; a democratic form of government of the people, by the people and for the people guided by the United States Constitution and by the people themselves - never by religion or sacred law. These values are basically American and I do not see how you can be an American without them.

Given these values, I am deeply disturbed by a religion in our midst whose sacred books contradict these American values and which seeks to install another set of values in contradiction to them. Not least of which is the notion or call for the death for Jews, Christians and other infidels. In other words, until I hear my Muslim neighbor adhere to the above mentioned values publicly and privately I shall consider him and his religion suspect and even subversive. No other religion but Islam has this call for the death of those who do not believe in its religion.

Normally it is repugnant for Americans to take an oath of loyalty and fidelity. The presumption is that anyone born in this country or who becomes an American through legal naturalization, gives complete allegiance to the United States. With one exception: the holy books of Islam - *Quran, Hadith, Sira* - which contain verse after verse of hatred and violence towards infidels (non believers in Islam) and other disturbing tenets. The *Quran* is the very word of God which cannot be changed, allegorized or reduced to parables but must be read literally. Americans refuse to address this grave conundrum between the American values and those of *sharia* but we must face it to be truthful to ourselves. We non Muslim Americans must have answers to the following questions and have the courage to ask them..

– He must forthrightly condemn all suicide bombers as inherently wrong and immoral because it kills innocents directly and intentionally.

– He must profess religious freedom of every person both for the individual and for the group as a basic right for all. This right includes the right to hold to any or no religion without being impeded by any secular or religious authority. This includes the right to leave any religion for any or no reason without coercion or violence.

    – He must hold to the equality of every person under the law whose ultimate authority is the United States Constitution and the people of the United States, not religion.

    – He must hold to complete separation of church/state whose guide is exclusively reason and history and never theology.

    – He must hold to the equality and dignity of the sexes in every respect.

These are values to which every American owes allegiance, before any religion or any sacred law. If someone can't adhere to each and every one of these values and on the contrary, wants to live by values directly opposed to them, such a person should not live in or come to the United States to make his home here. Better you go to a country that lives under those other religious values like many Muslim countries in the Middle East, South Asia and Indonesia. You do not belong in the United States of America. They simply are not welcome here. We should remember this simple proposition: *sharia* or Islamic law is contrary to every tenet we hold as Americans.

I do not know how else to say this honestly, forthrightly and sincerely. This is not from racial hatred or Islamaphobia but a simple statement of my basic values as an American which I am ready to honor and to defend to my very death. And to which I expect every loyal American to adhere to in heart and mind. God help me, I can do no other. As Abraham Lincoln said in 1858, this nation cannot live half slave and half free. The same can be said today: you cannot have two diametrically opposed value systems live side by side in America. Choose one or the other but you cannot have both democracy and *sharia*.

The next time you are engaged in a discussion (heated or otherwise) about Muslims, terrorism and Islam in this country and around the world, drop the discussion and ask these questions of any Muslim you are acquainted with. Depending on the answers, you will have a good idea about how much you can trust him or her. It will save you a lot of time, effort and frustration.

# CHAPTER 13

# OUR NECESSARY DIALOGUE
# WITH ISLAM

THE IGNORANCE OF AMERICANS about Islam is really hurting us as a nation. What we get are only bromides which are untrue: "Islam is a religion of peace" so as not to offend. We must recognize that no other religion welcomed to these shores has as one of its sacred doctrines Holy War - *jihad* - which is the mandated killing of Jews, Christians and infidels (those who do not believe in Islam). It is the only religion that consigns to Hell both in this life and in the after life, all non believers in Islam. The word "infidel" in Arabic means filth and refuse. This last view is theological in nature and hurts no one as long as it remains theological and not with a political agenda to enforce that belief on others, directly or indirectly. Islam is not a religion nor even a cult. It is a complete, total, one hundred percent way of life according to its religious law of *sharia*. This can be said of no other religion come to these shores: Buddhism, Hinduism, B'hives, Confucians, etc. -even atheism.

I should like to give some insights into this faith and its true meaning for the rest of us non Islamic believers so that we can be true to ourselves and to Muslims in this country and abroad about the nature and potential danger of this faith to all the rest of us. We must seek the truth or suspicion will only grow. Americans suspect that Islam is not a religion of peace. There are too many examples of Muslim killings around the world. With knowledge of Islam, they will know that it is not. This is not to be Islamaphobic (whatever that means) or racist but to be true to ourselves in knowing what this religion or ideology is all about. Islam has religious, political, economic, social and military components. The religious component is a wrap around for all the other components in a complete way of life..

It is difficult to engage Muslims in a true and in depth discussion of their faith because they refuse to do so outside of superficial explanations. They insist in showing us its rituals even its theology of *jihad* which is explained as a spiritual conquest of self.

To my knowledge none of the following is discussed or debated in an open free speech forum. We Americans simply refuse to face the reality of Islam itself so we fill our relationship with bromides (and untruthful bromides) about Islam being a religion of peace. Historically this has never been the case in the fourteen hundred years of Islamic history. On the contrary, Islam has been advanced by conquest of the sword and its thrust was stopped only by Christian fighters who fought to hold back the spread of this faith by force. Its heroes are Charles Martel

(732); Pope Urban II (1095); Isabella and Ferdinand (1492); Jan Sobieski (1683) and the end and ultimate defeat of the Ottoman Empire after WWI (1914-1918). Were it not for these Christian fighters, we would all be in mosques and under *sharia* law with none of the freedoms we enjoy today. Our freedoms stem from our Judeo-Christian culture. We owe these Christian heroes profound gratitude for saving our faith - with all the evils associated with those endeavors. Here are some basics of what Americans must know about Islam and which alone can be the basis of any true and authentic dialogue or understanding with that faith. We shall compare it with our own American values as contrast.

– As I have said, Islam is a total religion - not just a cult or ideology. Its component parts embrace every aspect of life. There is no separation of church and state (which follows from its ideology) and Muslims owe complete and absolute allegiance to *sharia* irrespective of any secular law to the contrary. They obey divine law not secular law. They obey secular law only when they are a minority. In reality, they hold to *jihad* mandated by Mohammad as a violent conquest of the whole world and by a slower, non violent Islamization when Muslims are a minority. Their demands increase with their increased numbers: less than two percent, they are a peaceful religion; two to five percent they begin to proselytize from ethnic minorities (e.g. blacks in American prisons); from five percent an individual influence; at ten percent lawlessness increases as in France and any insult to Islam is met with rioting, violence, etc.; at sixty percent there is unfettered persecution of infidels of all religions as in Sudan, Qatar, Malaysia and Albania. This Islamization therefore grows with the number of Muslims in a particular country. When they are only 0.6 percent as in the United States, they are regarded as a peace loving religion and religious "accommodation" is given to them by a tolerant and open society like the United States. For a true Muslim, there can be no real peace until the whole world is subject to *sharia* and submitted to Islam. That is why for Islam the whole world is divided between the House of Islam (where *sharia* rules) and the House of War (all other countries). This war may be violent (when Muslims are a majority) or non violent Islamization (when a minority). That is what war means. In both cases, the objective is all the same: submission of the whole world to *sharia*.

– Therefore Islam is not a religion of peace except by the propaganda to make themselves acceptable to infidels who are a majority and hold political and military power (e.g. the United States, Canada, Australia, etc). Muslim history proves this as well as the paradigmatic example of Mohammad who led armies of conquest in some seventy two battles (*hadith*). All Muslim experts in the jurisprudence of *jihad* hold that it is not a spiritual mastery of the self but a constant and complete holy war against all infidels until the whole world is subject to *sharia*. We saw how Muslims divide the whole world and only after the universal conquest of submission of all people and nations to *sharia* can there be peace in the world. Between the two houses there can only be a state of war, depending on their numbers whether it will be violent or non violent. This war may be violent when they have the numbers and power to do so; or by internal subversion, a form of Islam of a peaceful nature and accommodation to Islamic law and practices until they have the numbers and power to demand more and more "accommodation" (Islamization). The present assault on free speech by Muslims all over the western world is only the beginning (e.g. the fatwa on Rushdie after his book on Islam, the Danish cartoons of Mohammad followed by Muslim mayhem and killing all over the world and by the lecture of Pope Benedict XVI about Islam being a violent religion). This assault and its acquiescence by western nations (e.g. refusal to reprint those cartoons which made international news and were therefore news worthy) is a form of *dhimmitude* light, that is, the beginning of submission to Islam by the media because of fear.

– Most important is the fact that the values espoused in *sharia* directly contradict practically all the basic values of our American democracy which are as follows: equality of the sexes in all matters including the law; civil rights for all irrespective of sexual orientation; religious freedom to join or abstain from joining any religion or to exit any religion with no disabilities or violence; separation of church and state; inherent human rights in every person no matter what religion, sex, color, etc.; democracy and secular rule by the people who are the final authority in society not theology or religious law, etc. Everyone of these values is contradicted by *sharia* which simply cannot coexist with true democracy and secular America. In fact, any attempt to live by *sharia* in America is subversive of the United States and cannot coexist in the same place and in the same society. As Lincoln said in 1858, we cannot have a country half slave and half free, that is, two diametrically opposed value systems about the nature of man. This is perhaps the greatest danger internally to America *because these two value systems cannot be reconciled.* No amount of "let's just get along" can bridge this gap. Americans simply refuse to face this fact and Muslims refuse to discuss it - because its implications are so dire. It is like Hitler when he wrote in his *Mein Kamph* in 1938 that he was going to kill all the Jews in Europe - the democracies refused to believe it because it was too horrible to contemplate. The same can be said of the *Quran, Hadith* and the *Sura.* You can see this in the vehement denial of genocide committed by the Turkish Ottomans against the Armenians from 1915- 1918. Almost two million Armenians perished during that period while Turkey today vehemently denies this by saying that Muslims do not commit genocide. The evidence against Turkey is overwhelming. In addition, any creeping Islamization must be totally resisted *ab initio* and seen for what it is. We must have the courage to tell Muslims that if you live in America, you live by American values and if you wish to live under *sharia*, you should not make your home here. You should go to a Muslim country where *sharia* is law. And that is not the United States. Any attempt to subvert these American values with diametrically opposed values must be seen as an act of treason and must be resisted. Multiculturalism, that is, a co-existence of opposed value systems is not the American way. Lincoln put it well almost a hundred fifty years ago: this country could not remain half slave and half free. One or the other must prevail. We are confronted with the same choice today. We cannot live with democracy and *sharia* in any coexistence because both hold values and they are diametrically opposed to each other. What will it take to wake Americans out of their religious stupor? To make room in the same society with an opposite value system is a form of suicide.

– Islam does not hold to religious freedom. Any Muslim who leaves Islam and converts to another religion is to be killed according to the *Quran.* In an ideal Islamic state, "people of the book" (Christians and Jews) may practice their faith as long as they pay the tax of submission. In addition, they are made second class citizens with multiple disabilities in a state of *dhimmitude* to show always that they are inferior to Islam. This finally is not religious freedom at all as we know it. Religious freedom means to be free to practice one's faith without any interference from any other religion or secular authority (unless it goes contrary to the common good) and without having to pay any tax or suffer any disability because of its practice. We tolerate the changing of religion as a matter of conscience and violence may never be used to forbid it. Islam holds that it is right to use violence against those who convert. How can this be religious freedom? It is totally ironic that Islam in the western world and in

America is perfectly free to build mosques, schools and community centers and make converts in freedom while in Islamic countries there is no such freedom for Christians and Jews, only persecution, hate preachings and killings. There is no Islamic country that permits religious freedom as in the West. If there is no religious freedom, there can be no political freedom and that is why Muslim countries are so retrograde.

– Any dialogue between Americans and Muslims to be true and authentic must include each of the following requirements, that is, each and every one of them. They are really four basic requirements for any dialogue between Christians and Muslims.

1. A clear condemnation of all violence in and for religion such as suicide bombers (homicides). This must be forthrightly condemned because it is the killing of innocents. For Islam, there can be no innocents among infidels. They are all to be hated and killed. There can be no dialogue between Muslims and Christians without a condemnation of all violence in religion. That means the end of violent *jihad*. That is most difficult since it is a mandate of the *Quran* itself and has been sued for fourteen hundred years.

2. The violence against Jews (anti Semitism) and all *jihad* against Christians and infidels must completely stop. This is a real problem for Islam because there is so much hatred in the holy books of Islam against Jews - who are "descendants of pigs and dogs." This seems difficult to overcome since these holy books of Islam are reputed to come directly from God which cannot be denied, allegorized or neglected. A true Muslim can reject none of these anti Jewish and anti infidel commands of the *Quran* and is obligated by his faith to follow them. This is perhaps the greatest obstacle to ecumenism. Westerners never try to examine or face this conundrum.

3. The right to religious freedom is a fundamental human right which must be forthrightly affirmed by both sides of the debate. No religion has the absolute truth (only God does) so that all people must be permitted to practice religion (or no religion), change religion without any form of violence or disability. Of course, every religion has its own internal laws to deal with its members (but never by violence or with the help of the state). In Islam there is no "secular state" (they are one) so that *sharia* rules supreme. There is no secular law only a divine law that rules everything. It is either religious freedom for all as an inherent human right or any dialogue with Islam becomes very difficult not to say impossible. There is no Muslim nation today that permits religious freedom as in the West. Just the opposite is the case.

4. Each side must have respect for the good faith of the other. This really is a respect for conscience which is the voice of God given to each human being as a natural and human right inherent in the nature of each person. Even when we consider that the other follows an erroneous path religiously or morally (unless it affects the common good). The Islamic teaching that it is correct to lie to infidels to protect and promote Islam must be absolutely rejected for any true dialogue. Otherwise if we cannot speak openly, freely and truthfully to each other; how can there be any meaningful dialogue if we distrust the word of the other? That would be impossible. All of these four requirements for dialogue are absolutely non negotiable. And every one of them contradict *sharia*.

– Any criticism of other religions must be protected by free speech. While all conversation should be civil and rational and all forms of name calling, suspicion of others, accusations of racism or Islamaphobia (whatever that is) must not take the place of free speech in addressing each religion (or non religion) by each side. It is in the nature of free speech that nothing here is out of bounds unless it is vituperation, name calling, broad brush condemnation without rational content or foundation. The right to criticize each other's religion, its founder, its practice and its holy days, is subject to free speech and cannot be forbidden by "codes" limiting this basic right or by 'sensitivity' to the feelings of the other. As long as the criticism is truthful and though to be truthful with the other side having reasonable opportunity to respond and be heard, free speech must be respected. To call into question various Islamic practices (e.g. honor killing, cliterectomy, violence to those who criticize Islam like the famous cartoon imbroglio in Denmark, status of women, polygamy, etc.) is absolutely permitted by free speech. Free speech is the hallmark of any free society. Not to permit it or even to be intimidated because of it, is the mark of tyranny and fascism as it is today in Iran.

Americans need to have answers to these questions and holdings of Islam and not to gloss over them in order to live in peace or to utter bromides like "Islam is a religion of peace" when we know that it is not or refrain from criticism of the other out of 'sensitivity.' Any sincere dialogue with Muslims must forthrightly address these issues without being called Islamaphobic or be considered hatred of Islam. It is an effort to understand each other, Muslims and Americans, so that each knows where each stands without denial, obfuscation, name calling, fear of violence or simple animosity for asking these basic questions. To have any attempt to engage Muslims at this serious level has been met with charges of racism and Islamaphobia. Otherwise, suspicion of Islam will only grow to the point of disastrous steps taken to limit or even expel Islam from this country in case of another or even greater 9/11. Enough of the bromides: get down to serious discussion of these basic and fundamental issues where we both consider the internal holdings of Islam. Given the great amount of politically correct evasions, we can no longer avoid this very serious conversation and dialogue. If all the teaching in the *Quran* and *Hadith* (killing of infidels, hatred of Jews, *dhimmitude)* are all is for the last day, this would be only a theological belief with which we could live. Who cares? If however all this is to be implemented in the here and now - which is going on today all over the world by *jihadists* - then we have a really great problem on our hands which cannot be avoided or glossed over with rose colored glasses. Our whole future as well as the heart of our civilization is at stake - and nothing could be more serious than that.

As Bernard Lewis, the eminent scholar on Islam, put it, "In 1940, we knew who we were, we knew who the enemy was, [and] we knew the dangers and the issues. It is different today. W e don't know who we are, we don't know the issues and we still do not understand the nature of the enemy." That is why I wrote this book, that is, to make Americans understand the nature of our enemy and why we must fight or reject him. Look around, America. We no longer can state who we are, what we believe and why we fight. This is the result of relativism and multiculturalism.

We seem to be morally lost or in a sea of relativism, secularism and materialism. Islam is not.

That is why Islam is bound to win unless the American people awaken.

# CHAPTER 14

# THE ENEMY WITHIN: THE CASE OF MAJOR NIDAL M. NASAN

IN NOVEMBER OF 2009 after the slaughter at Fort Hood, Texas. President Obama asked Congress not to investigate the act of Major Nidal Malike Nasan. The President asked Congress not to investigate this massacre until the FBI has completed its investigation. It is ironic because it was the FBI who had all the information before hand and did nothing about Nasan. The FBI claims that there was not sufficient evidence to arrest Nasan which in light of all the evidence we have is a pure absurdity or a coverup. They had e-mails to an operative of AlQaeda (Awlaki); they had the testimony of Commander Mike Jacobs, U.S. Navy, who was a fellow student in a class of officers earning their masters on health care at Bethesda, Maryland for over four months; they had the knowledge communicated to them by uniformed superiors of that college; they had writings and emails by Nasan about supporting *sharia* and defending Muslims (the war on terrorism) who claimed a right to resist foreign invaders. In spite of all this, FBI officials after the massacre immediately said that the FBI did not consider the possibility of Nasan being linked to terrorism. In light of all this information which the FBI had of Nasan at the time of the shooting, the FBI was covering up either for their political correctness or simply lying to cover up their own incompetence.

Now the final report is in called "The Ticking Time Bomb" issued by the Senate Committee on Homeland Security and Governmental Affairs headed by Senators Lieberman and Susan Collins. Not once it is mentioned in that report about the background of Nasan's radical views on Islam or that his greatest allegiance is to his religion and not to the Constitution. In addition, each branch of the armed forces also released their reports with, again, no mention of Nasan's Islamic tendencies. All this despite Nasan's astonishing trail of Islamic fundamentalism that anyone could clearly see that he was a fundamentalist jihadist.

In addition to all this, there was the testimony of a Navy Commander Mike Jacobs who attended class with Nasan for four months at Bethesda, Maryland and whose testimony alone should have been enough to make the FBI and the army not only informed of all this Islamic background, but enough information to have heads roll at the top of the FBI and the military after the fact. None has. The families of those killed at Fort Hood have every right to know what happened at Fort Hood and the events leading up to that massacre and why those agencies civilian and military did nothing to prevent the greatest slaughter of United States citizens since 9/11. In fact, it can be called a second 9/11 which could have been prevented.

Here is the testimony from the FBI itself that is from analysts from a Joint Terrorism Task Force (JTTF) about communications between Nasan and an AlQaeda operative in Yemen:.

> JTTF ".... asserted that the content of those communications was consistent with research being conducted by Major Nasan in his position as a psychiatrist at Walter Reed Medical Center. Because the content of the communications was explainable by his research and nothing else derogatory was found, the JTTF concluded that Major Nasan was not involved in terrorist activity or terrorist planning."

The e-mails sent from Nasan to AlQaeda representative Anwar al Awlaki who had ties to the 9/11 hijackers and who had been investigated by the FBI twice and who had been detained in Yemen at the request of the U.S. government - were anything but "benign." What business does a United States officer have contacting a member of AlQaeda? That should have raised red flags.

The public does not know the details of that Fort Hood shooting and that civilian and military authorities could have stopped the massacre from happening by arresting Nasan. They did not because, in the opinion of Commander Jacobs who testified about Nasan, it was politically correct not to do so because of the negative effect this would have on American-Islamic relations; and that they would be accused of Islamaphobia. Fear superceded caution which resulted in a massacre.

Navy Commander Jacobs' testimony (which he personally communicated to me) testified to each of the following:

- Commander Jacobs and Nasan were in the same class about environment in reference to public health along with some thirty high ranking officers of various branches of the armed forces. They were studying for a Masters in public health.

– Nasan wrote inappropriate pieces for class about opposition to the war and about Muslims having the right to defend themselves against the United States forces.

– Nasan was directly asked by Jacobs: did Nasan believe that any conflict between the Constitution and *sharia* (Muslim holy law) that *sharia* should prevail? Nasan replied 'yes.' How could Nasan live up to his oath about defending the Constitution against all enemies foreign and domestic? Commander Jacobs received the following answer: Nasan's allegiance to the Muslim community worldwide was superior to any oath to the Constitution and that was his religious faith.

– Navy Commander Mike Jacobs reported all this to the military officials of the school on numerous occasions and nothing was done about Nasan.

In short, the FBI as well as high level military authorities all knew what Major Nasan was saying and what he wrote. There were so many red flags that should have made these authorities act before it was too late. They did not. The testimony of Commander Jacobs went a long way to reveal the real nature of what happened at Bethesda, Maryland, at the college. All this was done in the presence of many other officers in class who heard all the conversations between Nasan and Jacobs. Clearly one of those "regs" must be that any soldier/officer in the armed forces who speaks in favor of *sharia* or who opposes the war on terrorism on a consistent basis because it attacks Muslims or who claims his faith is superior to any other oath he might take, must be investigated as a matter of common sense. As we now know, Congress in its report and in the several reports of the armed services all failed in this respect by not even mentioning the whole Islamist background of Nasan.. It is frightening to think that there are other Muslims like Nasan in our armed forces.

# II

Therefore there was enough evidence to reasonably conclude that the shooter at Fort Hood, Texas, was a Muslim fanatic obeying the injunctions of the *Quran* to kill infidels who attack Muslims. Here is the evidence in its entirety.

– Malik Nadal Hasan was a born Muslim and an American. He was deeply religious.

– The testimony of another eye witness, Col. Terry Lee, ret. was enough to convict. He heard Nasan say "Muslims should stand up to oppressors." "Muslims have a right to rise up." "Muslims must resist aggressors in Iraq," "Maybe we should have people here in America to strap on bombs in the U.S." Nasan compared suicide bombers to American soldiers who threw themselves on grenades to save companions. While at Walter Reed Hospital, Nasan argued with wounded soldiers from the war about how wrong the war was. This was known by his supervisors at the hospital but they refused to take action as it would appear politically incorrect.

– Nasan did not want to go to Iraq/Afghanistan where he was to be deployed because he did not want to kill Muslims.

– There are precedents: S./Sar. Akbar of the 101st Airborne, a Muslims, deployed in Kuwait waiting to invade Iraq. There, he threw two grenades killing two soldiers of the 101st yelling that his Muslim people should not be killed. He was convicted and sentenced to death. Nasan's supervisor should have been on guard about Muslims who while in the army expressed opposition to the war.

– Nasan was perfectly sane, showing no signs of combat fatigue or stress. He methodically killed his fellow soldiers in a clearly planned attack. There were other eye witnesses who heard Nasan say the same things as did Colonel Lee including Commander Mike Jacobs.

– Nasan was seen executing his fellow soldiers with two guns purchased just days before. He gave away all his belongings before the attack which, he said to neighbors, he would no longer need. He expected to die as a martyr in defense of Islam.

– As Nasan fired, he was heard to say by witnesses at the scene, "Allah, Akbar, God is great!" It was the last cry of the nineteen hijackers during the 9/11 attack which is the signature of *jihadists* going into battle all over the world

– There is not only enough evidence to convict Nasan of murder but that he did it as an act of hatred toward those Americans who were being deployed to kill Muslims in Iraq or Afghanistan. His killing was in defense of Islam. Legal in *sharia*; illegal in American law. This would make him a martyr with a right to heaven.

Unfortunately much of the media for two days after the massacre even refused to refer to his Muslim religion. That was the mojo of most of the media in its refusal to study the very nature of the *Quran* and the silence of Muslims on this basic issue that faces them in the modern world. We either confront this question head on or we go right on ignoring the elephant in our front room. When every so often, Islamic violence crushes some Americans by American Muslims as it did at Fort Hood, the media always looks elsewhere for the cause, e.g. stress from the war. As long as we do not confront this basic question, the American people will simmer with hatred and suspicion of everything Islamic. This problem calls not for polite dialogue with good wishes and bromides, but for honest and direct confrontation.

**Conclusion**

Therefore the events at Fort Hood, Texas on November 5, 2009 were clearly a second 9/11: it was done by an Islamic dedicated Muslim; it was carefully planned for days with hand guns purchased for this purpose; it was an attack on United States soil against infidels (Americans) seeking as many American deaths as possible (thirteen deaths and forty three wounded); both 9/11 and 11/5 were begun like every attack of *jihadists*, in the name of God, *Allah Akbar*, which is the *jihadists'* signature both here and abroad. The American media was anxious to blame this event on the two wars in Iraq and Afghanistan and the American Islamic propaganda machine (CAIR) which claims that the attack was that of one aberrant and confused man who had nothing to do with Islam.. In fact, the shootings at Fort Hood had everything to do with Islam. This was not the work of a man under stress (he had never seen combat) but a planned religious attack in conformity with and in obedience to, the mandates of the *Quran* and in line with the fourteen hundred year violent tradition of Islamic war on the West in the likeness of Islam's paradigmatic example, Mohammad himself. Bin Laden must be very proud of the act as well as the stupidity of the American officials and the media.. None of this was narrated in the report "A Ticking Time Bomb" put out by the Senate Committee on Homeland Security and Governmental Affairs in spite of the overwhelming evidence of Nasan's own words and actions. Political correctness even in the armed forced was also responsible for the thirteen deaths at Fort Hood on that fateful November day.

# CHAPTER 15

# WE ARE AT WAR - LIKE IT OR NOT

IT IS OFTEN SAID that we are not at war with Islam but I think that Islam is at war with us. Islam divides the whole world into two parts: the lands of peace where *sharia* rules and the lands of war where *sharia* does not rule. We are in the land of war. An analysis of these terms will reveal Islam's reality here and now. Therefore Islam is at war with the United States which is overwhelmingly Christian and Jewish. This simply cannot be denied no matter how many times Muslims in this country claim that Islam is a religion of peace. It is or will be, says the *Quran*, only when the whole world is converted to Islam and not before. Until then, it is at war with countries which are infidels, i.e. the United States. Our American elites refuse to acknowledge this simple proposition.

There have been intense disputes over building a Muslim mosque/cultural center near the site of 9/11 where nineteen Islamic *jihadists* drove planes into buildings and killed almost three thousand Americans. Whatever American Muslims say - "they are not responsible," "they are not *jihadists*," "that is not Islam," etc. - no American can get it out of his mind that nineteen Muslims were responsible for that act of war. These Muslims who, like all American Muslims, read the same sacred texts and give them a violent interpretation. Which one is correct? In spite of American Muslim protests that they are not terrorists, it is up to them to show us that their interpretation of the *Quran* and other holy books is radically different from that of the *jihadists* - a very difficult task indeed. But how shall we know which one since all Muslims read from the same holy books and are sworn by the very will of God to follow and obey the directives of the *Quran* and the *Hadith*. By what right do American politicians make a distinction between a "good" Muslim and a violent *jihadist*? They have become Islamic theologians even if there is no Islamic theology.

In addition, the whole Muslim world knows the meaning of "Cordova" house as the mosque in New York City near 9/11 is called. It is or will be a replica of the third largest mosque in the world, celebrating the victory over Christians by the Moors in Spain in the tenth century and built over a Catholic church. The only ones who do not know this are the American elites and talking heads who in their liberalism treat this dispute as a matter of religious freedom and tolerance rather than a dagger thrust into the heart of the great Satan as its very name "Cordova" suggests. Historically, it can mean nothing else for Muslims all over the world.

In spite of all that the United States has done for the Muslim world - liberation from tyranny, protection from ethnic cleansing, massive economic help in natural disasters in places like Pakistan and Indonesia, even money to rebuild mosques; the United States is considered to be at war with Islam and nothing we can do can change that. This for two reasons:

The very doctrine of *sharia* that mandates war with infidels all over the world until the world is subject to Islam and God's holy law of *sharia*. The second reason is the two wars conducted by the United States in Afghanistan and Iraq, Muslim countries. There is no question that the United States considers itself at war with AlQaeda which is fundamentalist Islam. But Muslims from all over the world join the fight there including American Muslims.

For these two reasons alone, the United States is seen by the Islamic world to be at war with Islam. The reason for this, Muslims believe, is to insure the vital source of oil from the Middle East without which the American economy would crash. There is some truth in this because the supply of oil from the Middle East is in the vital interest of the United States. The second reason seems to be self contradictory. If we succeed in capturing or killing Bin Laden, this will be seen as the last straw in the Muslim world. That would show beyond doubt that the United States is at war with Islam in spite of all the ambassadors for peace sent by the United States government from the time of president Bush. Killing Muslims is killing the whole community of Islam which is one and which therefore makes the Muslim world so intensely anti American. The actions of Americans in Muslim countries seem to Muslims to be hostile for the purpose of assuring the supply of oil.

For these reasons it is difficult to conduct a rational dialogue with the Muslim world. Its schools, madrases, are not really schools but places where the young memorize the *Quran*. Why so?

Islam since the eleventh century has rejected the use of reason in theology and in analyzing the nature or the actions of God. There can be no real theology (reflection on the nature of God and his creation); therefore there remains only jurisprudence, that is, a study of the law of *sharia* of what it permits or what it rejects. That too is the use of reason but on another subject other than God (who is absolutely transcendent) and his creation since God does not create rationally. He is transcendent and above all rationality. The use of reason is thought to be hostile to Islam thus making it difficult to make a breakthrough to the Islamic world. When total truth is contained only in the *Quran*, compromise becomes impossible. Only between rational beings outside of theology can you have things like compromise, give and take, negotiation, etc. And there is more.

In the final analysis, fondly do we hope, fervently do we pray that American forces not find or kill Osama Bin Laden. If that happens, it will be the greatest recruitment tool in the Islamic world second only to Mohammad himself. Bin Laden is perhaps the most admired man in the Islamic world because of his heroic resistance to the infidel in the cause of Islam and Allah. Kill him and you will have a hundred million recruits. His death shall have been one of martyrdom of the very first order. He is seen as the modern Saladin to free Islamic lands from the infidels. If we think we have a problem with the Islamic world now, that will be nothing in comparison when and if we kill Osama Bin Laden. Tens of thousands of Muslims will join Bin Laden's *jihad* as one sent from God to restore the glory of the Islamic world and its faith. That shall have been a sure sign of holy war for Islam against the West such as not seen since the uprising of the Machti in nineteenth century Sudan. We will then have a true war between civilizations whose outcome is difficult to predict. As they say, be careful of what you wish for because in getting it, our present plight will be seen as minor compared to what awaits us.

All this together makes dialogue with Islam virtually impossible especially when the other side considers itself at war with you: also consider the lack of reason, the vital need for oil in the West, the hero of the Muslim world, occupation of Muslim lands by infidels and what will happen if the allies succeed in capturing or killing Bin Laden. While not yet perfect, what we are witnessing is a revival of Islam on a global basis for which the western world is not prepared to deal with. President Obama again and again tries to mollify the Middle East and its Muslim population by friendly gestures but anti western feeling among Muslims only increases. In fact, Obama in not standing up for his own values which is seen as weakness as a strong horse versus a weak horse, in the words of Bin Laden. Instead of preparing the American people for the coming storm, Obama tries to mollify our enemies with little success. He even refuses to consider military action against Iran before Iran develops a nuclear weapon. This may well be the final piece in the failure of United States foreign policy.

We are at war and it is a religious war. This realization has not yet dawned on the American people and certainly not on liberal elites. To put it clearly, any Muslim is welcome here, may pray and worship as he pleases and hold any theological position he wishes. He may seek to convert any willing subject non violently. However, any Muslim who wants to live by *sharia* and its commands must not make his home here and if he does, he will be held in grave suspicion because *sharia* is absolutely incompatible with American values and American law.

# CHAPTER 16

# ISLAM AND CHRISTIANITY: THE CONTRAST

THE ARGUMENT IS OFTEN made that since Islam and Christianity both have their roots in Abrahamic monotheism, that makes them similar because they both come from the same root of Abraham. Muslims make this argument mostly in the West where they are a minority (but never in Muslim countries) where they want to be accepted . They would like very much to take their place along side of Judaism and Christianity as the third great Abrahamic religion in America.

Nothing could be further from the truth. The basic values and principles of United States documents come from the Bible not from the *Quran*. The differences between the two faiths of Islam and Christianity are so profound that just because they both come from the same monotheistic root, that fact does not make them in any way similar. In short, in all the basics of their respective faiths, the gulf is so vast between Islam and Christianity that we can say that they are radically different; and being radically different, they have almost nothing in common

I should like to compare these two religions without trying to make one better or worse than the other. That choice will be up to the individual to choose and decide. What we can do is to show the radical differences between the two faiths and let everyone choose for himself. Consider the following;

1. In *Christianity*, God is love essentially through and through. He is not loving because his very nature is love. Forgiveness, compassion, mercy belong to his very nature and he must exercise these virtues accordingly because they come from his divine nature. In *Islam,* God is beyond all categories so that we can know nothing of God's nature. He can be merciful and forgiving but only if he chooses to be so.

2. In *Christianity*, God loves all men and desires their salvation and by his grace leads them to the truth. God rejects no one and seeks out ways by his grace to save all men and to be with them. In *Islam*, God only loves Muslims and rejects and hates infidels who have rejected Islam. All men must be converted to Islam or they are going to hell.

3. In *Christianity*, God beckons all men to come to him freely and never uses force or coercion to do so. Salvation is offered to all men and women but they must freely choose to accept that salvation. In *Islam*, force may be used to convert men to Islam. That is the very

meaning of *jihad* in the *sharia* which has been part of Islam from its beginning some fourteen hundred years ago. If people reject Islam, it is because of bad faith and they can be killed as infidels and then they will go to hell. This is what one Muslim scholar says of violent *jihad*: "*Jihad* is in defense of and the spread of Islam.... it is *jihad* for the sake of Allah. Moreover, there are religious scholars who view *jihad* as the sixth pillar of Islam." Sheik Wajdi Hawaet al-Ghazwi, in a sermon at Mecca on October 6, 2001. .

4. In *Christianity*, God calls us freely and he must have our 'yes' even for our own salvation. There is therefore no predestination or force in Christianity. God gives freely but men must respond freely. Man remains free to accept or reject God's call, to take his own fate into his own hands. *Islam* is a determinist religion. Everything is by the will of God which cannot be resisted and will necessarily come about no matter what we do

5. In *Christianity*, every person is endowed and created by God with inherent human rights so that every man and woman are equal in this sense. All men and women have human rights which must be respected by everyone and by the state. In *Islam*, the fulness of human rights belong properly only to male Muslims because they are better than all other peoples. Other men and women do not have natural rights which Muslims must respect.

6. In *Christianity*, God is love, therefore he is Father and we are his children. We are destined to become one with him in eternity and salvation lies in union by love with God by his holy grace. There is an intimate relationship between men and God to the point where men participate in the divine nature. Eternal life is spiritual in nature and union with God is brought about by love. In *Islam*, all these terms of intimacy and union with God as Father participating in the divine nature are all blasphemous. We cannot come close to God and our heavenly reward remains (in eternal life) terrestrial in nature: things which we have in this life but magnified many times over: fine foods, the best wine, beautiful women.

7. In *Christianity*, there is a serious attempt to be ecumenical, understanding other religions and to accept the fact that other religions have elements of truth which Christians must endeavor to find and respect. Christianity does not have the absolute truth even if its truths remain true; only God is absolute truth; in fact, we can learn from other faiths. All peoples may be saved if they believe in God and follow their conscience by doing good and avoiding evil. *Islam* alone claims to have the fullness of truth and other religions are only lies, deception and works of the devil. Other religions cannot have elements of truth because Islam alone has the fulness of truth. Outside of Islam, there is only untruth and eternal damnation.

8. In *Christianity*, God is three yet remains one called Trinity. God has but one nature, one being, one will but three relationships who are one in all things except in that relationship. They are Father, Origin without Origin, Son begotten of the Father from all eternity and Holy Spirit who is the loving union of Father and Son. In *Islam*, all talk of Trinity, God's Son is blasphemy because God is absolutely eternally one. Islam calls the Trinity and those who believe in the Trinity a form of polytheism. Christians are polytheists. God is one, absolute, almighty and unknowable. We may only worship God but we can never be united with him. God is merciful but only if he wants to

9. *Christianity* mandates love of all men and women, even of enemies, because God loves all men and women as his children. They must love even enemies because they are children of God and endeavor to help them in any way they can. Love must characterize every action of the Christian. They must love sinners and forgive them their sins if they repent sincerely.

In *Islam*, Muslims must love only their fellow Muslims and hate all the rest. Muslims must particularly hate Jews because they are no longer the chosen people. Muslims must seek to kill them as well as all infidels any chance they get unless they convert to Islam. This hatred of enemies is mandated many times in the *Quran* and by its preachers all over the Muslim world.

10. The *Christian* must never lie under any circumstances. The lie is always forbidden even if his or her life is dependant on it. In *Islam,* Muslims may lie to infidels to protect and promote Islam as well as to save oneself from persecution and death. The lie is an instrument of Islamic religious propaganda

11. Every *Christian* is free to leave the church, the faith and the practice of that faith with no consequences. No force or coercion must ever be used to keep one in the faith just as God will not use force on anyone to enter the faith. In *Islam*, no one may leave the Muslim faith under penalty of death. If a Muslim joins another faith or church, he may be put to death by any of the faithful. One is not free to leave Islam. This would be to turn one's back on truth.

12. *Christians* may defend themselves only when they are unjustly attacked or invaded. This is known as the just war theory . The Christian may fight or use violence only in a defensive war, never an aggressive one. For the protection and promotion of *Islam*, any and every means of violence may be used and whatever is at hand. This violent *jihad* is incumbent on every Muslim male (when possible) for the protection and promotion of Islam and it is contained in the *Quran*.

13. In *Christianity*, all women are equal to men in every respect before the law and must be respected as equals. Marriage is only between one man/one woman. Christianity is strictly monogamous until death of one spouse. In *Islam*, women may be beaten under certain circumstances; they are not the equals of men in many respects of religious law. Muslim men can practice polygamy up to four women but not women (polyandrous) and only men may grant a divorce to a woman which for the male is as simple as pronouncing it three times in the presence of witnesses.

14. *Christianity* knows no specific social or economic law under which Christians must live. Democracy, socialism, free enterprise, capitalism are all compatible with this faith as long as social justice is assured, particularly for the poor and human rights of all are respected. In *Islam*, all Muslims must endeavor not to live under secular law but endeavor to live under Muslim law.

15. In *Christianity*, there is a clear division between church and state with each acting in its own independent sphere. Some conflict between the two sometimes comes about when civil law contradicts divine law; but generally one does not intrude into the jurisdiction of the other. Christianity has no political agenda and Christians are free to elect the government they desire to rule over them by secular law. The people are the final arbiter of the law in a democracy: "We the people in order to form a more perfect union...." In *Islam*, there is always union of church and state and it has a clear political agenda which is to convert the whole world to Islam. Muslims must live under sacred law (*sharia*) and there can be no separation of church/mosque because God rules in heaven as on earth. Democracy and ultimate rule by the people is incompatible with Islam except as a practical matter and only divine law is applicable to all things, public as well as private.

16. In *Christianity*, all men and women are equal before the secular law and with no discrimination before an impartial judiciary applying secular law. No religion or religious law

can ever tell the state what to do or not to do. That is the prerogative of the people. In *Islam* infidels and women are not equal before the law. Adulterers may be stoned to death along with homosexuals; thieves must have their limbs removed for theft while every criticism of Islam or Mohammad is punishable by blasphemy laws by imprisonment or death in many Muslim countries; women are to receive less in inheritance than males and their testimony is worth less than that of a Muslim man.

17. In *Christianity*, religious freedom is guaranteed to all religions or to none. Neither the state nor any religious group may use violence or coercion to convert others to the faith unwillingly. This is guaranteed under the First Amendment to the Constitution. Government must respect all religions but be neutral in its attitude toward all religions. In *Islam*, there is hardly any religious freedom in any Muslim country. Since Islam has total truth, how can there be religious freedom? Islam divides the world into the lands of Islam and the lands of war where violent *jihad* may be used to make those lands Muslim. No Muslim country has any law or constitution guaranteeing religious freedom to everyone. In fact, the *Quran* forbids it and no secular law may contradict the *Quran* in any Muslim country. Religious freedom is incompatible with Islam.

18. *Christians* may travel everywhere unimpeded by law or government. Non believers may enter their churches, even the most sacred ones and are encouraged to do so. In *Saudi Arabia*, on the contrary, no other religion but Islam is even permitted and only Muslims may enter the sacred cities of Mecca and Medina under penalty of death for unbelievers. Few churches are permitted in Muslim lands while mosques are freely built everywhere in the West where Muslims are free to worship, propagandize, build mosques and schools...

19. In *Christianity*, men and women may worship together as a family; they may attend church together and women must dress modestly but are not bound to dress in any particular way. In *Islam*, Muslims strictly separate all men and women everywhere: in schools, in mosques, etc. They may not pray together as a family unit but are separated in mosques.

20. In *Christianity*, in the holy books of the New Testament and the teachings of Jesus, there is not one word of hatred or death for those who do not share their faith. On the contrary, Christians must love one another and do good to and love enemies as well. Not one word of violence, coercion or hatred of others is contained in the New Testament. In *Islam,* the *Quran* is full of violence, death and hatred of Christians, Jews and other infidels and the killing of unbelievers. The one who converts from Islam to another faith is to be put to death

21. In *Christianity* men and women are both created in the image and likeness of God, i.e. the more they love, the more they become like God. In *Islam*, men and women are only created to worship and obey God under the sacred law revealed by Mohammad called *sharia* which rules every aspect of life both private and public. There is no likeness of God in man

22. In *Christianity*, freedom characterizes the Christian message and while Christians have historically failed in this respect in the past (Crusades, Inquisitions, Witch trials, persecution, religious wars), they have apologized for this and have determined in their sacred documents (Vatican II) never to resort to force in religion ever again. In *Islam,* there is only one freedom and that is to accept God's law and follow it. Even the "freedom" to leave Islam for another religion is punishable by death. .

23. Eternity in *Christianity* while intellectually obscure - "we see through a glass darkly" - remains as a form of union, a relationship of love because that is who God is. Eternal life and rewards in *Islam* are terrestrial in nature, only multiplied: good wine, beautiful women, fine

foods, etc. Eternal life is restricted to Muslims while all the rest of unbelievers are destined for hell.

24. In *Christianity*, the practice of abortion, euthanasia, embryonic stem cell research, cliterectomy are all forbidden. In *Islam*, abortion, euthanasia, embryonic stem cell research are also forbidden. But many Muslims practice cliterectomy on their young girls to make sure they are virgins at marriage. Muslim women may never marry infidels. Muslim men may marry infidels as long as their children are brought up Muslims.

All of these contrasts show the radical differences between Islam and Christianity. If there is one overriding characteristic in the two faiths, it is freedom or lack thereof. That is what makes the West so superior tot he Muslim world ; the freedom to choose. Only in the West may one choose freely which religion he or she will follow. This simply is not true in the Muslim world.

# CHAPTER 17

# JESUS AND MOHAMMAD

It seems strange that people who should know better tend to make all religions the same. The founders of religions are the exemplars *par excellence* for their followers and it is they who establish the basic principles which their followers are to be guided by and obey. They manifest the type of God they worship by their teaching.

These principles are as radically different in Jesus as they are in Mohammad so much so that we are viewing two different images of God. The principles enunciated by these two founders are based squarely on their view of God which makes their views foundational both as regards their faith and their view of God. This is extremely important because it tells us what kind of God we worship and why we worship him. Consider each of sixteen insights drawn from the foundational texts of both religions.

**How Should We Treat Our Enemies?**

- "Love your enemies and pray for those who persecute you." *Matthew* 5:44
- "Against them [enemies] make ready your strength to the upmost of your power, including steeds of war, to strike terror into the hearts of the enemies, of Allah and your enemies, and others besides, whom you may not know but which Allah knows." *Quran* 8:60

The two attitudes are incompatible. One is love, the other is fight and strike your enemy down. One is love, the other is killing. These qualities proceed from the nature of both Gods.

**How To React In The Face Of Attacks By Your Enemy?**

- "If anyone strikes you on the right cheek, turn to him the other also." *Matthew* 5:39
- "Will you not fight someone who broke their solemn pledges and prepared to drive out the messenger and did attack you first." *Quran* 9:13
- "The hour is coming when whoever kills you will think he is offering a service to God.: *John* 16: 2

- "Fight those who do not believe in Allah and his messenger, nor acknowledge the religion of truth, even if they are people of the book...." *Quran* 9: 29

The *Quran* teaches to give as you are given in retribution for one who attacks you unjustly. Or simply do nothing and not resist the one who attacks you in the Christian view. One is very human, the other is radically different.

## What Really Do You Do To Your Enemy When He Hates You And Rejects Everything You Are And Do?

- "Blessed are you when men revile you and persecute you and utter all kinds of evil against you falsely on my account. Rejoice and be glad, for your reward is great in heaven." *Matthew* 5:4
- "And slay them wherever you find them, and drive them out of the places whence they drove you out....." *Quran* 2:191

One is to rejoice in persecution of the name of Jesus while the other is to retaliate in the same way that you were given offense by your enemy. Fight or not to fight are answered differently in both religions. One is very human; the other radically different.

## How Shall We React Against Those Who Reject Us And Do All In Their Power To Eject Us?

- "And when his disciples James and John saw it [rejection], they said, 'Lord, do you want us to bid fire come down from heaven and consume them?' But he [Jesus] turned and rebuked them." *Luke* 9:52-55
- "May the hands of Abu Lahab perish. May he himself perish. Nothing shall his wealth and gain avail him. He shall be burnt in a flaming fire and his wife laden with faggots, shall have a rope of fibre around her neck." *Quran* 111:1-5

Those who reject the words of each follower are treated radically different. One bids a call for freedom; the other bids for vengeance and death for not listening to the words of the prophet.

## What To Do With An Adulterous Woman?

- "Neither will I condemn you. Go and sin no more." *John* 7:53-8:11
- "And she was put in a ditch up to her chest and he commanded people and they stoned her." *Muslim* VO 3, BK 17, no 4206

Adulterers were to be stoned as in the Old Testament which is the law of the prophet. Jesus forgives and refused to stone because we are all sinners. The one who has not sinned must be the first to throw the stone.

**What Are Their Respective Attitudes On Killing?**

- "You have heard it said to the men of old, 'You shall not kill and whoever kills shall be liable to judgment.' But I say to you that anyone who is angry with his brother shall be liable to judgment...." *Matthew* 5:21-22
- "Therefore when you meet the unbelievers in fight, smite at their necks; at length when you have thoroughly subdued them, bind a bond firmly on them...." *Quran* 47:4

Killing is forbidden by the former (we are even bidden not to be angry with the brother) while the second approves of killing infidels everywhere. The *Quran* is full of instances when it is proper and just to kill. Nowhere in the *New Testament* is there such a teaching. Not once.

**Who Is To Be Saved And How?**

- "God so loved the world that he gave his only begotten Son that whoever believes in him should not perish but have eternal life." *John* 3:16
- "Allah has purchased of the believers their person and their goods; for their in return is the garden of paradise; they fight in his cause and they are slain...." *Quran* 9:111

Once again God is pleased by belief in his Son in the *New Testament* while Islam is to conquer by slaying and being slain in which case paradise is for the slain and booty for the victors. The basic characteristic of Islam is violence and death in the spread of the faith..

**Perhaps The Most Characteristic Of Both Followers Is The Presence Or Absence Of Violence/Death In Bringing About Belief And Conversion**

- "All who take by the sword will perish by the sword." *Matthew* 26:52
- "Know that paradise is under ths shades of swords." (*Jihad* in Allah's cause)
- *Bukhari*, vol 4, book 56, no. 2818
- "Mohammad is Allah's apostle. Those who follow him are ruthless to the unbelievers but merciful to one another" *Quran* 48: 29

One need not repeat what has been said throughout the contrast of the two followers *supra*.

**What Kind Of Preparation For The After Life?**

- "Blessed are the peacemakers for they shall become sons of God. Blessed are those who are persecuted for justice's sake, for theirs is the kingdom of heaven." *Matthew* 5:8-10
- "Allah assigns for a person who participates in holy battles in Allah's cause and nothing   causes him to so accept belief in Allah and in his messenger, that he will be recompensed by Allah......" *Bukhari,*   vol. 1, book 2, no. 36

Any peacemaker is the Son of God. In Islam, the warrior who kills and is killed in battle is the one who is rewarded richly by admission to paradise. To be killed and to kill for Allah is pleasing to God. Nothing like this appears in the New Testament which favors forgiveness. .

**What Happens To Those Who Do Not Believe?**

- "Blessed are the merciful for they shall obtain mercy..... For if you love those who love you what reward do you have....?  *Matthew* 5:7, 46-47
- "Mohammad is Allah's apostle. Those who follow him are ruthless to the unbelievers but Merciful to one another." *Quran* 48:85

Jesus admonishes us to love all, even enemies and those who do not believe in him. Mohammad shares mercy for only those who believe. For him, others are to be treated without mercy.

**What Of Unbelievers?**

- "The hour is coming when whoever kills you will think that he is offering service to God." *John* 16:2
- "Fight those who believe not in Allah nor the last day nor hold that forbidden which has been forbidden by Allah and his messenger; nor acknowledge the religion of truth even if they are people of the book until they pay the *jizyu* with willing submission and feel themselves subdued."  *Quran* 9:29

This is the *jihad* to be fought until the end of time or until the whole world is subject to Islam and its holy law. The  followers of Jesus are simply not to resist evil men, even those who want to kill them.

**In The Propagation Of Faith, How Are The Followers To Conduct Themselves?**

- "My kingdom is not of this world; if my kingdom were of this world, my servants would  fight." *John* 18:36
- "I have been ordered by Allah to fight against the people until they testify that none has the right to be worshiped but Allah and that Mohammad is the messenger of Allah." *Bukhari*, vol. 1, book 2, no. 25
- Once again, the relationship between believers and unbelievers is radically different in both religions and cannot be  reconciled. We can see this most clearly in the following passages.
- "And if anyone will not receive you or listen to your words, shake off the dust from your feet and leave that house or town."  *Matthew* 10:14
- "Whoever changed his Islamic religion, then kill him."  *Bukhari*, vol. 9. Book 88. No. 6922
- "None of you will have faith till he likes his Muslim brother what he likes for himself." *Bukhari*, vol. 1, book 2, no. 13

If one kills a Muslim it is as if he killed all Muslims. This does not apply to infidels who should be killed. The golden rule in Islam is restricted only to Muslims.

## What Did Jesus and Mohammad Teach About Our Relationship With God?

For Jesus, God is Our Father who loves us and created us to be with him forever in love: "Our Father who art in heaven." God is the merciful God who seeks the sinner to return to him. He is the good shepherd who seeks what is lost no matter who the lost person is. Jesus taught us that we must love one another and even enemies and those who persecute us. God's desire is that we join him after death in a union of love. Such intimacy is foreign to Islam and all these attributes are considered a form of blasphemy. Eternity for Jesus is union with God who is love, one with the Trinity.

For Mohammad, all appellations of God are beyond our intelligence and the qualities of love, mercy and forgiveness are exercised only if God desires to do so. God loves only Muslims and hates those who have rejected Islam as infidels. His followers may even kill infidels who are all consigned to hell unless they convert to Islam. Islam's God is vengeful, vindictive; the only obligation of man is to worship God and follow his holy law. Eternity is an extension of this life and its fruits. There is no union with God.

## What Did Jesus And Mohammad Teach About Freedom?

Throughout the gospels, man is free to accept or reject the teachings of Jesus. There is no threat if one rejects this teaching and the disciple of Jesus is free to accept or reject this teaching. Force may never be used for people to believe.

Mohammad's God threatens all those who refuse to accept Islam by encouraging his followers to kill infidels. Any Muslim who leaves Islam for another religion is to be killed by any faithful Muslim. Man has only one obligation which is to worship God and obey his holy law. This is the only freedom in Islam.

– "The Jews say Allah's hand is chained? May their own hands be chained. May they be cursed for what they say. By no means. His hands are both outstretched: he bestows as he wills" *Quran* 5: 64

## What And Who Is The Word Of God?

Jesus is the Word of God who existed for all eternity with the Father and the Spirit in a relationship of love and gift. Since God is love, there must be a relationship between persons and not simply a solitary potentate. Jesus is the incarnation of God in the flesh who teaches us who God is in and by his very humanity: "And the Word was made flesh and dwelt among us."

All talk of intimacy of union with God, Father, Son, Spirit, incarnation are all rejected by Islam and are blasphemy and polytheism We can know nothing of the nature of God because he is transcendent and beyond all concepts and thought. Mohammad taught that God is One, Transcendent, to be obeyed and follow his sacred law. Nothing more than that. Even salvation is not guaranteed unless one dies as a martyr defending Islam or its spread throughout the world in a *jihad*.

## What Is The Final Word On Jesus And Mohammad?

Christians believe that Jesus is not dead but alive in and through his death and resurrection.

This was a conquest over death for all men who would believe in Jesus as resurrected Savior. The kingdom of God has begun now.

The teaching of Islam on Mohammad is that Mohammad is dead and awaits the final resurrection to eternal life which is a form of earthly reward, e.g. best wine, virgins, fine food, etc. In Islam, Jesus was a prophet who could not have been crucified and put to death (that was another in place of Jesus). As a prophet Jesus pointed to the coming of Mohammad, the last and greatest prophet who announced the final revelation of God which is Islam.

**Conclusion**

These are only a few passages from the sacred writings of the two founders of Christianity and Islam. The difference in attitudes to fellow believers, enemies, unbelievers is so radical between Jesus Christ and Mohammad (the *New Testament* and the *Quran*) so as to give us an altogether radically different God in each religion. They worship two different Gods. It is up to each member of the respective faiths to choose but he/she should know that the choice is between two irreconcilable Gods.

# CHAPTER 18

# IS THE UNITED STATES A CHRISTIAN NATION?

IT IS OFTEN SAID that the United States is a Christian nation and that while other faiths are welcomed, they must understand that America was established as a Christian nation by Christians. Well, yes and no. Clearly the overwhelming number of Americans are Christians, about eight five percent. But this alone does not make the United States a Christian nation as we are not ruled by any Christian or canon law but by secular law. In reality, we are a secular nation whose very first amendment to the Constitution guarantees that the government - state and federal - will not establish any one religion or give any one religion any special help or consideration. It has been an American tradition that while there is separation of church and state, the government is not hostile to religion and respects every religion while favoring none. Therefore the United States is a secular state which favors no religion and is friendly to all religions and to no religion. In this sense, the United States is not a Christian nation.

But to say that the United States is a secular state establishing or favoring no particular religion but is friendly to all, does not tell us the whole story. The reason why some are prone to call the United States a "Christian nation" is that the principles on which this nation was founded are essentially derived from the Christian faith. That is important to remember because these values cannot be replaced or changed without changing the very structure, operation and nature of the United States. Conceivably we could constitutionally change that value system (as some Muslims wish to do ) into one that reflects a particular religion which some countries do. We could change the Constitution to read that henceforth religious law would govern our actions, e.g. *sharia* or Islamic law. Islamic communities in Canada and England for example have petitioned the government for permission to set up religious courts headed by Islamic jurists, to judge Muslims in those countries under Islamic law and not under secular law. This of course would be the destruction of the unity of this nation as well as the end of the equality of the secular state. There really is no compatibility between a religious law and a secular state. This has been rejected outright in both countries.

What are some of these values, Christian in origin and nature, which form the basis of the law, government and mores of the United States? Consider the following *seriatim*:

*Separation of church and state* Christianity was the first religion in history to make such a separation. "Give to Caesar what are Caesar's." Therefore the religious and the secular power are separate and one may not subvert or usurp the power of the other. Of course there have historically been times in the past that one or the other has tried to usurp the power of the other but the reality is that these two powers are separate - which is not true, say, of Islam when all is governed by sacred law given by God. There are not two powers but one. Separation of the two powers in Muslim countries has never been the case until forced upon them by western colonial powers. All secular powers before Christianity combined the secular and religious orders. The emperor was *pontifex maximus*, the bridge builder between earth and heaven.

*Equality before the law* Every person is equal in reality and in law because they are children of God: rich/poor, men/women, educated and non educated/ religious or non religious. All are judged before the same law, before a neutral judge and none are privileged. This is not true in Islamic countries where only Muslim males are equal before the law and where women and infidels are not equal. In the democracies, each citizen is entitled to vote for those who would govern him. "We hold these truths as self evident that all men are created equal....." The foundation of those rights is not the state but God. "*Quod omnes tangit, ab omnibus opprobetur*" - what touches all must be approved of by all.

*Human rights* are enjoyed by every human being and each has his or her own dignity. As put in the Declaration of Independence: "We hold these truths that all men are created equal and that they are endowed by their creator with certain inalienable rights...." It is not religion or the state that gives men equality, rights and equal dignity, but God himself. Government is created in order to insure and protect these rights, equal in dignity and respect. In Islamic law, only Muslim males have human rights while others do not. These are usually incorporated into legal civil rights such as in the U.S. (Right to free speech, religious preference and freedom, corporal integrity, right to work, sexual equality, right to travel, to marry, etc.). These human rights in the United States are translated into civil rights by law. But the basis and foundation of rights is God himself who created all men. Thus the act of creation made all men equal and endowed them with these inalienable rights.

*Religious freedom* This is basic in American law. No one can be forced to belong to any religion or to remain in any religion which he or she sees as erroneous. In Islam, anyone who tries to leave Islam to join another religion is subject to death. In the Christian dispensation, God does not coerce or force. This is a basic Christian holding.

*Secular law* Not only is there equality before the law but the law is secular in nature. No one who is not a Christian may be judged by religious law. In fact, America is a secular society which is manifested by the separation of powers, secular and religious. The temporal affairs of a society are judged by secular law by an independent judiciary. Each faith may judge its constituents as it sees fit within its own religious realm but no others.

*Women are equal to men in all respects* This is a direct Christian teaching begun by Christ himself who subjected men and women to the same marital laws, the same commandments, the same privileges of men. Other religions have disabilities for women in many respects (e.g. testimony in court and in inheritance).

These six characteristics are only some of the values and principles which govern the United States and are at their roots Christian in nature. So that when we say that the U.S. is a Christian nation, what we are saying is that the foundational principles of the structure of American law, government and dignity of the human person in America are Christian in inspiration and origin and cannot be understood without reference to the Christian faith. This is true of no other religion in its influence on the United States of America.

# CHAPTER 19

# MUSLIM MOBS WHO DESTROY AND KILL OR MUSLIMS WHO HAVE INTERNALIZED THEIR ISLAMIC GOD

As an American I am deeply troubled by the violence and murder committed by Muslim mobs every time they think or perceive that Islam has been insulted. This trouble is doubled when we see those Muslim mobs in Afghanistan looking for Americans to kill because of the burning of the *Quran* by a church in Gainesville, Florida. When the mobs did not find any Americans to kill, they turned on the United Nations and killed seven members *who were there to help the Afghanistan people build their society*. The Americans in Afghanistan are there spilling their blood and treasure only to be singled out for death because of some non lethal act Muslims find offensive. These mobs seek to take it out on Americans in Afghanistan for something they had nothing to do with. This is beyond outrage. It goes to something in Islam itself which is corrosive and demeaning.

This is not the first time such murders, rape and violence by Muslims has taken place all over the world when they thought their religion was "insulted." Here are a few examples:

– A few Danish cartoons in the Danish press caused Muslim violence all over the world.

– There were Muslim riots after an erroneous report of the *Quran* being flushed down the toilet (unsubstantiated) at Guantanamo prison in Cuba.

– When Pope Benedict XVI pointed out that Islam seems to favor violence for any insult, there were riots all over the Muslim world killing scores and threatening the life of the Pope himself. He simply pointed out that violence cannot be associated with religion. He got his answer from Muslims.

– The present riots by Muslims have killed over thirty innocent people because a church in Florida put the *Quran* on trial, found it guilty and burned it. This was a continuing riot by Muslims several months ago when the same church threatened to burn the *Quran* but did not do it then.

– There were riots in Afghanistan a few years ago when a Muslim converted to Christianity and was condemned to death by a *sharia* court. The issue was "solved" by the United States who repatriated the man and his family to Italy. This is democracy in Afghanistan for which we fight?

– A woman teacher in Pakistan was jailed for blasphemy for permitting a student to name a teddy bear Mohammad. Another Christian woman in Pakistan was condemned to death under blasphemy law that was thought to be an insult to Islam brought about by the simple say so of one Muslim.  In addition, there are constant attacks on Christians in Pakistan all the time.

– There has been a continuous assault on Copt Christians in Egypt for unproven accusations of hiding a Christian woman who wanted to become a Muslim (a complete fabrication). This violence and killing has continued even after the fall of Mubarak as it was before Mubarak.

– Muslim operatives in Iraq have succeeded in attacking Chaldean Christians by killing them and burning their churches. Most of these Christians have moved out of Iraq where they have been for two thousand years.

– There are many more violent attacks on Christians, e.g. in Pakistan, the West Bank, the Philippines,  Indonesia, Nigeria, Egypt and Algeria (e.g. where seven Trappist monks who were all murdered by Islamic elements).  All these incidents amount to a veritable war on Christians all over the Islamic world even as Benedict XVI has time and again preached no violence in religion.  Violence on behalf of religion is a complete contradiction in terms. God forces no one to believe or not to believe as an utterly free act. It is men who kill to believe. But that is a Judeo-Christian view of God and religion which is not the view of Islam. That is the crux of the problem. The Islamic God is very much into violence, killing and vengeance. Here is a sketch.

The very spread of Islam has been by the sword and conquest which Mohammad called *jihad*. Mohammad himself participated (according to *Haddith* which has as much authority as the *Quran*) in some seventy two battles for the spread of Islam. This conquest was an injunction from God laid upon every male Muslim to the degree possible and in each situation which presents itself.  For Islam, the world is divided into two groups: the lands of Islam where *sharia* governs (*sharia* is the codification of the *Quran* as the divine law); and the lands of war where *sharia* does not yet rule.  Between them there can only be war (*jihad*) either by violent means or by Islamization until the whole world is submitted to *sharia*. Conquest of lands is not the important dimension in Islam; it is the universal submission to God's law which is the core of Islamic conquest.  That is why lands once Muslims can never be given back to the infidel, e.g. Israel, Spain, parts of Italy, etc.

Secondly, the very nature of the commands in *sharia* are diametrically opposed to democratic ideals such as those values in the United States: equality of men/women; monogamy; religious freedom for all under the protection of a neutral state which favors no religion but protects the basic right of conscience vis-a-vis religion or even no religion; that is, religious freedom for all; separation of church and state; secular law for the common good administered by a secular judicial system without reference to any theology or religions law.  All this insures the freedom of all to worship in any religion he desires or in no religion; to conduct his life in any way his conscience chooses; to conduct his own life in his own way with no *dictat* from any religious or secular authority.

In *sharia* there is but one freedom and that is to submit (e.e. Islam) to God's holy law. After that every aspect of one's life is directed and governed by that law: familial, political, social, sexual, culinary, in short, there is no personal freedom except under *sharia* which directs all activities down to the minutiae.  This is really the closing of the Islamic mind to anything new or progressive which remains as primitive and backward as in the seventh century which is considered the ideal era, that is, the greatest era to be imitated and followed. The rejection of reason in the eleventh century insured this closing of the Muslim mind in anything new or progressive, including reason. There can be no progress in such a situation and under such a religion.

The third and most important thing to understand the reason for the highly violent reaction by Muslims when Islam is attacked, "insulted" or simply opposed. Non Muslim people (infidels) are cursed by Allah for whom only hell awaits them. The Allah of the *Quran* is vindictive, violent against unbelievers, vengeful and totally un-ecumenical. The followers of such a religion should and must imitate the nature of such a God who is merciful but only if he desires to be. The nature of God can only be revealed to man only by God (since God is beyond all names, all laws, even his own word is not incumbent on God because he is absolutely transcendent and free).

What does the *Quran* teach us about the nature of God which is determinant on all his followers? That God is one and there is no other God; that anyone who denies this is cursed and condemned to hell unless before death he converts to Islam; that unbelievers are to be hated, mistrusted and killed by every means possible; that Allah is a vengeful God who injures, kills and condemns all those who oppose him or do not believe in him; that only Muslims are to respect each other since all the rest are condemned to hell in the afterlife; that one need not be respectful of any infidel (meaning garbage) or treated as equals; that the infidel should be killed if possible and never to be made friends with unless to take advantage of him for purposes of conquest; and that a good Muslim may even lie to an infidel in order to promote or protect Islam. Islam has nothing to learn from any other religion since only Islam has the fullest of truth. If any truth exists in other religions it is because it already exists in Islam and in its holy books. Finally, it is therefore natural that if any Muslim leaves Islam to join another religion (or no religion) he must be killed for having turned his back on the only truth there is - Islam. In short, Islam worships a God who hates. *It is normal that his followers follow suit because they have internalized their God.*

When you put all this together, you begin to understand why Muslims react with violence and even murder when they perceive that Islam has been insulted or threatened (which leads to the same thing). When this is done by infidels (e.g. the church in Florida burning the *Quran*) it becomes a terrible insult to Islam which must be avenged in the name of God *because God is a vengeful God on unbelievers.* One cannot forgive or be merciful to the perpetrator of the insult or attack. He or she must be put to death because he has blasphemed, that is, insulted the one true God in his holy Word.

One simply cannot imagine a violent-revenge by Christians or Jews if the Bible or the Torah was burned. There would of course be protests but not violent ones. That is because Christians are mandated not to harm enemies but to forgive them. *The God of Judeo-Christianity is a completely loving and merciful God who is the God of all men and women who are all made in the image and likeness of God.* In the words of St. John, "God is love and those who inhabit love, inhabit God." Love is his very nature. Christians must act in accordance to the nature of their God. In Jesus, not a word of vengeance and hatred against those who do not believe in him or even reject him. He forgave and prayed for those who killed him. That is in marked contrast with all those Muslim mobs when they feel that others have insulted Islam because that is the vengeful nature of their God which they must follow.

In this view of the nature of God in Islam, we can begin to understand the violence and revenge Muslims feel when they think that God is insulted and humiliated by the burning of God's very word. This act is one of the gravest sins possible because it is like burning God whose word the *Quran* really is. Those mobs of Muslims react violently because that is the way their God has commanded them to act against the infidel. Reason, compromise, tolerance are all useless words in the face of an insult to Islam by burning the very word of Allah, that is, Allah himself. *The nature of God determines the acts of his followers whom they wish to follow in every respect.* To burn the *Quran* is really to burn God himself and that is the highest form of blasphemy which simply cannot be permitted..

Hence the murderous violence against those who are perceived to insult Islam in the burning of the *Quran* in Gainesville, Florida. The nature of God determines the actions of the ones who worship him. Muslims have internalized the Islamic God who is a God of vengeance and hatred of infidels.

# CHAPTER 20

# RELIGION AS SOURCE OF VIOLENCE

BOTH IN THE MEDIA and in public opinion, the cliche is that religions do not lead to peace but to war. This is particularly true of the three monotheisms: Judaism, Christianity and Islam. This for three reasons

– When one defends one God, the adherents are intolerant of those with many gods or with none. When you believe that there is only one God, those of others are false gods.

– Monotheism demands of its adherents to convert others (proselytizing). We then go from proselytizing to intolerance which is an easy transition.

– Finally, the God of Judaism, Christianity and Islam is a dominant God who makes believers submitted peoples, obedient peoples - even fanatical peoples for orders which they believe come directly from God. For many, religion and sect in the bad sense, is one. What can be said in the face of these three accusations that religion has produced more violence than peace?

The map of religion in the world - not their territories of diverse religions or the number of the faithful but their vitality and their capacity for expansion is as follows.

**Secularism and the European Existentialism**       In four of the five continents, religions are present, living and active not only in private life but also in the public forum. In many countries, there is no separation of church and state as in the United States. There is one exception: Europe.  All European countries and the U.S. have separation of church and state.  All have in their constitutions a form of separation of church and state. The countries of Europe are secular in nature so that to organize their societies collectively they have no reference to God or transcendence or any sacred traditions but pretend to be governed by reason alone and by the rules of law and values defined only by man. This attitude  is really less than two centuries old.

There is yet another map showing the places where there are wars and violence against the rights of man (genocide) and those countries where there is peace, democracy and the observed  rights of man. We should remember that even in Europe, religious peace is recent. Ireland until recently was embroiled in armed conflict between Catholics and Protestants because of the dominance of Protestants. There are deep religious roots in the conflict in Kosovo and Serbia (is it more nationalism or religion?).  Bosnia had to be divided because

Christians and Muslims were killing each other. When the Americans withdraw, the killing will begin again.

In other words, in many cases religion comes to reinforce ethnic differences. In Russia there is Islamic Chechnya but the objective of the conflict is political even if Islam is involved. They want to be an Islamic nation. Other former republics of the old USSR have political difficulties but have nothing to do with religion. In Asia there is a lot of violence: in India, Indonesia, Philippines and Sri Lanka - all have nationalistic and religious problems. One uses the other. In India, fundamental Hinduism re-informs Indian nationalism and uses violence against Christians and Muslims. In Africa, the conflicts are religious and ethnic in nature but there is religion mixed up in Nigeria, Egypt, Darfur, Somalia, Ivory Coast and Senegal. In Rwanda (1993-95) the genocide of Tutsis by Hutus, Catholics on Catholics which implicated bishops and priests. There the problem is tribal and ethnic not religious. In Iraq, there is a confrontation between Shiites and Sunnis. And there is the Israeli-Palestinian conflict which has become more and more religious with the terrorist Hamas in Gaza in the south and that of Hezbollah in the north. The same in western China where Chinese Muslims want a separation. Consider occupied Tibet which has both ethnic and religious differences between the Han Chinese and the Tibetans.

**Violence Has Complex Origins**     An important part of terrorism is ethnic, nationalistic and political violence which seem to have roots in religion. But the situation is complex. Terrorists are not all Muslims even if most terrorists are Muslims. There are Christian, Hindu, Buddhist terrorists. And terrorism is not always religious. For example, the violence in the Basque in Spain is not religious. Neither is the Shining Path in Peru. Nor the terrorists in Sri Lanka. Whenever there is violence, the situation is usually complex. South Africa remains one of the most violent countries in the world but not for religious reasons. Up to independence, it was ethnic and racial differences between white and black. And if we examine the places where there is peace we find that religions are often instruments of peace and reconciliation. Violence plays little role in those places. The media seem to show only the places of religious violence and not where religion promotes peace.

### History of Christianity: Cathedrals and Crusades

Much is made of violence in the past of Christianity and Islam. On the Christian side there has been anti Semitism, inquisitions, crusades, burning of heretics and witches and wars of religion. In Islam there is the corporal punishments for certain crimes, the inferior position of women, the general absence of the rights of man and expansion by violence and warfare called *jihad*. The rights of man are hardly present in Hindu and Buddhist religions because of the lack of solid conception of the person.

Like all the monotheisms of the world, Christianity has a long history. It has become a civilization and a world wide culture. It gave birth to empires that endured for centuries with whole bodies of literature, knowledge, technology and works of art. It related to billions of men and women throughout the ages. Who says civilization says a whole mixture of history of great things and villainy, faults and crimes committed by religious peoples. The history of religion covers centuries and millennia. In Christian countries their history is both crusades and cathedrals. There is a mixture of good grain and weeds. More of this later.

**The Combat of All Generations**     In the internet age, the whole world is a global village. We judge everything by our standards. We think we are better than our forefathers. Yet the

United Nations Declaration of Human Rights dates only from 1948 and the rights of man dates from 1776 and 1789 - only two centuries ago. We think that we are better than our ancestors. Hardly. Consider the following: WWI and WWII, the Holocaust, the massacres of USSR and China, Cambodia, Rwanda and Congo. We are no better than our fathers. Perhaps worse with modern nuclear technology whose potential destruction is global. We have our own weaknesses such as torture, victimization and ethnic cleansing. Violence is present throughout the world today and the mystery of evil remains. We are not innocent and we can hardly blame former generations. This violence is everywhere today. The struggle for peace, religious and secular, is a combat for all generations.

**Comparisons** What is really telling is when we compare the three monotheistic religions in their holy books and the attitude and teachings of their founders. *Judaism* has a problem since the Old Testament is filled with holy wars, violence and killing to expand the kingdom of King David and others such as Solomon, Ashatz, the Maccabees, etc. Conflict continues today with Israel and its neighbors.

*Islam's Quran* is filled from beginning to end with violence, the killing of infidels and Mohammad's teaching of *jihad* all contained in the codification of the *Quran* called *sharia*. It will be difficult to separate holy war from these basic teachings in the Islamic sacred books and the history and attitudes of Mohammad.

In *Christianity*, all of the holy wars, Crusades, inquisitions, etc. are all aberrations from the New Testament where there is not one word about holy war or killing to spread the faith or of taking up the sword. A return to the teachings of the New Testament will insure that Christianity will remain a peaceful religion as it was for some three hundred years at its origins.

**Note On Christianity** The New Testament and the example of Jesus are completely non violent which rejects all forms of violence, revenge, threats of violence, hatred, etc. Jesus' teaching is all voluntary and entail no threats even if they are rejected. "If you wish" is a constant theme in the gospels which is the mark of freedom. No one may be forced to believe in or come to Christ, contrary to some of the later history of the church. The first three centuries of Christianity were centuries of non violence, non resistance, following the example of Christ who threatened or cursed no one, even those who unjustly murdered him: "Father, forgive them for they know not what they do." Jesus' teaching goes beyond the law, never contrary to the law. "You have heard it said thou shall not kill. But I say to you not to be angry with your brother." "Love your enemies and do good to those who hate you so that you may be like your Father in heaven...." When Jesus was slapped by a guard during the passion, he did not threaten. And when Peter strikes back with the sword to protect Jesus, Jesus rebukes him and commands him to put up the sword. Thus the example and teaching of Jesus are non violent and the command never to use violence even to save one's own life.

Later centuries will not follow the example of Jesus, especially when they came to support the state. The Middle Ages still tried to attenuate the violence of man with the truce of God, immunity from violence for certain groups and places, sanctuary but never a resort to pacifism in the example of Jesus. Only in more recent times have elements of Jesus' teaching on non violence been once again part of the teaching of the church: rejection of capital punishment, just war theory, conscientious objection sanctioned by Vatican II, no violence in religious matters. In the words of Benedict XVI, there must be no violence in religious matters. The church seems to be returning to the practice of the early church in matter of violence and coercion.

**Note On Islam**     The problem with Islam is the very notion of God and its holy book, the *Quran*. The *Quran* is the very word of God which every true Muslim must follow and be obedient to. It contains all sorts of barbarisms (stoning for adultery, death for Christian and Jews, holy war (*jihad*), cutting off limbs for theft - and much more.) The whole concept of God in Islam is one of hatred for non Muslims, a God of vengeance, etc. It is often said that there can be no peace between Islam and the rest of the religious and secular world until Islam's view of the nature of God is changed.

None of this negates the aberration of violence in the history of all three monotheisms. But only Christianity can be shown to have so seriously deviated from the teachings and attitudes of its founder and its way back is remarkable. Judaism remains in the tradition of Israel and Muslims are commanded to *jihad* or holy war to protect and spread Islam and *sharia*.

**Note On The Crusades**     There are different forms of crusades. Those against diseases, poverty and injustice  remain good because they are all signs of the presence of the kingdom in our midst but will be completed by God on the last day.. After 2001, President Bush spoke of the global crusade against terrorism - good against evil. Many reject this formula because of its bad history during the Middle Ages.

The word 'crusade' started in the eleventh century of armed Christian groups going to free the Holy Sepulcher in Jerusalem called by Urban II in 1095 at Clermont, France to deliver the holy places in Jerusalem (which fell to the Muslims in 1078). This war was declared for religious reasons and considered both as a penance and a plenary indulgence given for the forgiving of sins which were granted to anyone who participated in it. The Crusaders wore the sign of the cross on their uniforms  to designate this religious motive: *Crux* = Crusades.  In good faith Christians believed that salvation resided in Jerusalem.  But above all, it was for the purpose of stopping the forward conquests of Islam against the West which was not really completed until 1683 at Lepanto when Muslim armies were stopped permanently. The present surge of Islamic terrorism is a revival of Islam's holy war.

**Holy War**     From the beginning, the Crusades were considered a holy war. It was justification of violence for religious reasons, that is,   to defend Christianity against the invasion by Muslims (Bernard of Clairvaux). This violence by Muslims was exercised against all that was not Islamic. The Crusades began by massacring Jews in 1095 in the Rhine valley.  In the thirteenth century there was the Crusade against the Albigensians (*Cathari*) in the south of France.   While terrible things were done by the Crusades, they were defensive wars against advancing Islamic armies to stop that forward thrust and to save Christianity. It succeeded at Lepanto with the defeat of the Ottomans.

The idea of taking up arms to defend Christianity appears strange to us today.   Ten centuries later, after colonization and the conquest and forced conversion of Indians, two world wars, the Holocaust, etc. it appears that the very term "Crusade" can no longer be used in the name of any religious defense. Many writers refused to give Franco and the Spanish Civil War (1936-1939) the name of 'Crusade.' Eisenhower called WWII a crusade against the Germans. Dictatorships were supported by the Catholic Church for too long. The word "crusade" no longer belongs to Catholic vocabulary of today but it simply cannot be denied in its historical context and its unpleasant effects. Still there remains violence in the name of religion - terrorism, *jihadism*, suicide bombers, etc.  As to Christians, the argument in the

West is that there must never again be violence in the name of religion. Conversion must be free or it is just another form of tyranny.

**Conclusion** What have we learned in the evolution of violence and religion? Five points:

– *Every person has a natural right of freedom of conscience* to follow any or no religion which he or she has seen as true and wants to follow and adhere to that religion or to none.

– *Since religious freedom is a matter of conscience,* it belongs to the freedom of each person to follow his/her conscience and under no circumstances can he/she be forced or coerced to follow a religion, to believe in any or no religion or to be obliged by force or threat to remain in any religion. He may leave or adhere to any religion freely. Violence in matters religious is utterly forbidden as a direct attack on the integrity of the person.

– *Every religion has elements of truth* within it and we are morally obliged to try to discover the truth therein contained (at least partially) in every religion. This gives rise to true and authentic ecumenism. Inter religious dialogue is therefore a moral obligation for peace and mutual understanding.

– *The state may not favor one religion* over another and must be neutral, protecting religious freedom for all. This clearly implies a separation of church and state since the state has no competence in matters religious. The state must insure the freedom of all citizens to follow their conscience within the context of the common good.

– *Religious tenets that disturb the common good* may be restrained or forbidden to that extent: e.g. killing of innocents, polygamy, use of hallucigenic drugs, participation in fraud as an economic scheme, etc.

# CHAPTER 21

# THE BASIC QUESTION IN OUR WAR ON TERRORISM

MANY AMERICANS ARE BEGINNING to wake up to the internal threat which is Islam. The danger is now internal as well as external as Islam tries to do from within what they could not do from without. That is, Islam has been trying to conquer the western world from the Balkans to the rest of the world for over one thousand years until the Ottomans were defeated at Lepanto in 1683. The present Islamic fundamentalism all over the world is a continuation of that conquest mandated by Mohammad and the *Quran*. What Muslims could not do by military conquest, they are attempting to do internally in America and Europe by massive immigration. Europe already has thousands of mosques and as much as seven percent of the population. Since most Muslims refuse to integrate into the culture and the values into which they have immigrated (multiculturalism), they tend to live by themselves and by their own culture which is under the holy law of *sharia*. This coupled with a high birth rate assures their future as Muslims in Europe.

In Islamic immigration, there are two insurmountable problems for the West. First, a clear refusal to live by western values and therefore under western culture. Secondly, a willingness to live only by Islamic culture under *sharia* which is the codification of the *Quran*. This is deemed to be the very word of God which cannot be allegorized or denied. Any Muslim who refuses to live by *sharia* is no longer a Muslim but an infidel (e.g. filth, refuse). But he may cover it by *takiyyah* or deception.

Recently in Europe, Prime Minister Cameron of Great Britain, Prime Minister Angel Merkel of Germany and President Sarkozy of France have all pronounced multiculturalism unworkable because it does not integrate itself into western culture and its values. That is, western culture is incompatible with *sharia* and the values espoused therefrom. As Prime Minister Cameron put it, this Islamic multiculturalism is a refusal to live by the following values which are essentially Judeo-Christian and western:

- human rights for all
- democracy
- social integration
- equality before the law

To be a true Englishman or German or French (as well as an American) is to live by these values which are really derived from the Judeo-Christian tradition. Islamic multiculturalism really denies those values and desires to live by Islamic values which are diametrically opposed to the above stated western values. That is what I mean when I say that the West's struggle is now both within western countries as well as with the struggle with Islam abroad. In other words, it is a conflict of values which many Muslims living in the West refuse to accept. These western values are: human rights for all, religious freedom for all, equality before the law and the equality of women, separation of church and state, secular law and democracy. These values are diametrically opposed to Islamic values contained in *sharia* to which every Muslim is sworn to uphold and live by under penalty of unbelief. Hence the deep problem for Muslims who have immigrated to the West. It is true that Islam commands obedience to the law of unbelievers when they are a minority. But this is only to last until Muslims are a majority when they must live under *sharia*. That is what Cameron, Merkel and Sarkozy are talking about: a refusal to truly accept and live by western values. Multiculturalism cannot produce true Englishmen, Germans, or Frenchmen or Americans. All three western leaders have loudly and publicly proclaimed that multiculturalism is a failure and can no longer be acceptable or permitted. That poses a real dilemma for authentic Muslims living in the West and in the United States. It was the Prime Minister of Australia Julia Gillard who more bluntly put it: if you come here, you must live by our values (western) and if you do not wish to do so, you should not come here (Australia). Every western nation must make the same statement and enforce it on all. It is either that or it is suicide for western culture by this internal menace.

The struggle with Islam and Muslims in the West is a struggle over values which make authentic Americans, Australians, Englishmen, Frenchmen and Germans. It is as simple as that. Muslims must not come to these countries if they do not wish to live by the values of those countries. And they must not try to obey *sharia* by multiculturalism. Otherwise it is a lie which is permitted to Muslims by *takiyyah*. Multiculturalism is dead because it has failed to absorb those essential values in the West. Any attempt to live by different values and therefore by a different culture is both unacceptable and treason to those western countries.

Now that is what we are talking about in this war on terrorism which is really about radically different cultural civilizations. Liberals in this country simply refuse to accept this simple proposition. One is derived from the *Quran* and *sharia*; the other is characterized by values derived from a Judeo- Christian culture. The two are radically different and cannot coexist in the same place at the same time. Prime Minister Gillard of Australia said it best: if you do not want to live by our values (Judeo-Christian values), you should not come here; and if you are here, you [Muslims] have a fundamental choice to be made: live by the above enumerated western Judeo-Christian values and culture and absorb them into your life style; or leave this country and go where you can live *sharia* in peace and tranquility. But the one thing you may not do is to come to western shores and try to live under Muslim *sharia* values with or without the cover of *takiyyah*..

The decision will be tremendously difficult for Muslims here and abroad. In Muslim countries the overwhelming number of Muslims wish to live under *sharia* because they are a majority. Muslims in our country must make a choice and they cannot have both. It is either *sharia* or western values. That is the problem today with Muslims in our midst. A Muslim cannot be a real Muslim without allegiance to *sharia* as the very word of God; and an American cannot be an American without allegiance and dedication to Judeo-Christian values come down to us from Judaism and Christianity. We Americans seem afraid to pose this basic question directly to Muslims in our midst: *Do you adhere to values of sharia or to those of the Declaration of Independence*? Bromides like "Islam is a religion of peace" will not do. "A house divided cannot stand."

# CHAPTER 22

# MURDERED MIDDLE EASTERN CHRISTIANS: OUR FUTURE

AFTER THE MASSACRE OF Christians in Baghdad, in Egypt, in the Territories, in Turkey, in Indonesia and in Pakistan, religious leaders in America who call for tolerance for Muslims in the West, must insist on tolerance as a reciprocity all over the Muslim world. Otherwise it's all pure hypocrisy. Our religious and secular leaders are quick to plead for tolerance of Muslims in the United States but they are almost silent about the many atrocities against Christians in the Muslim world. Such a massacre of Christians is an attempt at religious cleansing by fundamentalist Al Qaeda Muslims which can no longer be tolerated. Muslims from around the world have given hardly any protests. Consider if a Christian had entered a mosque, any mosque in the world, and killed scores of Muslims as they prayed. The whole Muslim community would have demanded expressions of regret and sorrow as well as condemnation from the whole non Muslim world from the Pope on down. Indeed what we hear from pulpits all over the Islamic world each Friday is hatred for Jews and Christians as filth (i.e. unbelievers). These condemnations reiterate all the way from Mecca to London to the United States. Clearly it is such hate speech and hate sermons that result in killing and death of Christians. What else are we to think when five hundred Muslim clerics in Pakistan approve of the assassination of a Muslim governor whose only crime was to defend a Christian woman sentenced to death for Islamic blasphemy. It should be remembered that blasphemy in Pakistan is defined as what any Muslim person considers offensive to Islam. No other proof is necessary. This is pure hatred of Christians and other non Muslim minorities. Muslims want to religiously cleanse their countries of non Muslims (e.g. Jews and Christians). And consider the *fatwa* from the greatest Muslim university in the world in Cairo speaking to hundreds of millions of Muslims, that decided that it is legitimate to attack and kill non Muslims anywhere in the world. This gets no mileage in the western press which is now awash in commentary and analysis about an insane person who killed six people in Tucson, Arizona. But when millions of Americans are threatened with death in the name of Islam by Islam's most prestigious university in Cairo which influences millions of Muslims all over the world, this receives no real press coverage. Pure insanity for our national security.

The reality which the West must face is that it is impossible to live under both Islamic *sharia* law and the values of liberal democracy. There are over a hundred passages in *sharia* law that call upon Muslims to kill Jews, Christians and non believers. The conclusion to such a law is that one who believes in such a law (and since it is the very word of God which cannot be spiritualized but accepted literally) is a clear and present danger to all non Muslims and should not be admitted to the United States. *No other religion in the world calls for the death of those who do not believe in their religion.* Only Islam. And that is because *sharia* commands it. It is now time for leaders in the West to say simply and loudly along with the Prime Minister of Australia, if you believe in *sharia* you are not welcome here. That is not a question of freedom of speech and travel but a question of the safety, security and survival of the American people. How can we live with a religion that threatens us with death? Why is it so difficult for some Americans and American leaders to understand this?

We must once and for all examine the nexus between Islamic doctrine and the murder and mayhem committed by Muslims all over the world, particularly on Jews and Christians - *as advocated by the holy books of Islam.* This is the very crux of the problem and the basic question which should be asked of all Muslims. If all this was to happen at the end of time, we could all live with that. It would only be a theological doctrine. Unfortunately that is not the case as all Islamic jurisprudence teaches: *jihad* and *sharia* are for now in th example of Mohammad himself.

Given the fact that there is only one Islamic doctrine that comes from the *Quran*, any one who follows this doctrine (*sharia* is only a codification of the *Quran*) is a danger to us all. There really are no "moderate" Muslims; only those who believe and follow *sharia* and those who do not. Those Muslims who desire the establishment of *sharia* here and abroad cannot have it both ways: you believe in *sharia* or you believe in democracy. The two cannot co-exist. In 2007, the University of Maryland joined with the pollster World Public Opinion to survey Islamic views. These included Muslims from throughout the Islamic world. Two thirds said they would endorse the requirement of "a strict application of *sharia* law in every Islamic country." This is a view shared by over half of Indonesian Muslims, a country thought to be "moderate". In Pakistan, four out of five favor strict enforcement of *sharia*. Therefore implementation of *sharia* is held by hundreds of millions of Muslims throughout the world even if they do not actively promote it themselves. But *sharia* lies there like a loaded gun for any Muslim who takes seriously its mandates. There is no moderate or immoderate Islam; there is only Islam as written in the holy books of the *Quran* and the *Hadith*. The real problem is therefore Islam itself along with its holy books which must be taken literally and not spiritually or metaphysically. If this is true (and according to accepted Muslim doctrine it certainly is), then the source of terrorism is Islam itself in its holy books read literally by Muslims. *Sharia* is hostile to our civilization and those Muslims who believe in it wish to destroy it by the imposition of *sharia* law which is a direct contradiction to the values of democratic constitutionalism. Why is that so difficult for our leaders and intellectuals to understand this once and for all? It is exactly like those westerners who refused to believe Hitler when he wrote it down in his book *Mein Kampf* of what he was going to do when in power. It was too terrible for the West to believe because it was too preposterous that he would kill all Jews. Just as today our leaders refuse to believe that Islam desires our destruction when it is there written in the *sharia* law. Unless there is something of a radical change or evolution of this Islamic law. In fact, there is not a chance of this as it has not been for fourteen hundred years of Islamic history which has been one of violence and conquest by Islamic armies originally led by Mohammad himself. This hope of such an evolution is a very slender reed to depend upon.   Muslims who believe in *sharia* must not be allowed to immigrate to the United States. . How can you be tolerant of a religion whose holy books threaten non Muslims with death?

Once again, there is no moderate Islam, only Islam as written in its holy books. We must have the courage to admit it, confront it and oppose it no matter how much we are accused of war with Islam. To that extent, we must be and are at war with Islam. We in the United States cannot live with *sharia*. The West has no stomach for this so it repeats the bromide that Islam is a religion of peace and that we must be tolerant even of texts that seek to destroy us and our civilization. It seems that this is a desire for suicide for the West.  This comes from extreme tolerance in the West which is no where practiced in the Muslim world.  Remember what *sharia* stands for: the inequality of men and women; death to adulterers and homosexuals; amputation of limbs for theft; no separation of church and state; diminished status for Jews and Christians (*dhimmitude*); no democracy and rule by *sharia* that governs every act of every person both private and public. All these values are diametrically opposed to democratic constitutionalism. *Sharia* requires and demands the destruction of the freedom of the West. For this there must be a return to the Islam of the seventh century to escape modernity with all of its corruptions and allures for Islam which can only lead to a rejection of Islam itself. Such a rejection of modernity is at the core of the survival of Islam. That is why Bin Laden wants everything western removed from Islamic lands. Moderate Muslims are not moderate because they do not believe in *sharia* law (one cannot be a Muslim without allegiance to *sharia* law) but because they do not believe in violence to bring it about.  But the objective of moderate and fundamentalist Muslims is the very same (or they would not be Muslims).  One group wants to spread *sharia* law all over the world by any means including violent means, the other by slow, peaceful means called Islamization as is happening slowly in the United States and in Europe.  But the object is the same: imposition of God's law which is *sharia*. The difference is in means and not in goals.

In short, Islam is not just a religion.  It is also an ideology that controls every aspect of public and private life ruled by *sharia* law.  As we have seen, this law is opposed to all the values which we Americans hold dear: democracy, equality, freedom of speech and action, separation of church and state, secular law administered by impartial secular judges, women's liberation, etc. - all diametrically opposed to *sharia* law.. This conclusion is clear even if most Americans and our political leaders simply refuse to accept this.  So they are satisfied with bromides "that Islam is a religion of peace" when fourteen hundred years of Islamic history prove just the opposite.  There is a call for tolerance of this religion in our midst.  But tolerance for a religion whose holy texts advocate our killing and destruction of our way of life? This is very difficult.  That is a tolerance for our suicide not for Muslims to express themselves freely. We must wake up before it is too late. All those decimated and murdered Christians throughout the Islamic world today are proof of what awaits us when and if Islamists ever come to power. Islam desires a religious cleansing of the whole world.

# CHAPTER 23

# ISLAMIC WAR ON CHRISTIANS

TODAY IT IS THE supreme irony that Islam has managed to turn the tables in the western world. It is politically correct to emphasize and condemn any discrimination of Muslims in the West as Islamaphobia; and while scores of politicians and clergymen in the United States come to the rescue against discrimination of a minor religion in American called Islam; at the same time, it is politically incorrect to mention that Christians are being killed wholesale and imprisoned throughout the Muslim world by Muslims. Muslims have managed to make westerners believe that the West - "crusaders" - have declared war on Islam; whereas in reality it is Islam that everywhere in the Islamic world (and beyond) that has declared war on Christians and for which we have a clear record to prove it. Americans protest discrimination against Muslims while the same American Christians refuse to protest the killing of thousands and thousands of their fellow Christians by Muslims. It seems to be a one way street: protest against rather minor discriminations against Muslims in the West (e.g. France forbidding the nibab) while not hardly a word of protest of wholesale slaughter of Christians by Muslims all over the world.

One has only to look at the record of the past twenty years. Benedict XVI keeps on preaching that there must be no violence in religion even while he witnesses the killing of thousands of Christians by Muslims everywhere in the Islamic world - and he says nothing so as not to antagonize Muslims further. As when he gave a speech in Regensburg speaking the truth that Islam has historically been a violent religion. For that, there were riots by Muslims, killing scores of innocent people and threatening the life of the Pope himself. And he apologized! *The historical record of the past twenty years has been war on Christians by Muslims all over the world and no violence against Muslims by Christians in retaliation.* And yet we hardly hear a word of protest by the Christian community in the West, particularly from the churches in Europe and the United States. Only the Prime Minister of Australia has said it loud and clear: if you want to live under the Muslim law of *sharia*, then don't come to Australia. If you come to Australia, you must live by our values and traditions not the laws of Islam. Make up your minds. You came freely to Australia. Now you have a right to leave if you can't accept Australian values. Can you imagine any American president (Obama?) ever saying such words for America?

That Christian protest should be about the *Quran* itself as the very word of god that calls for the killing of Jews and Christians in many of its passages. There is nothing of this in the

New Testament which is full of forgiveness and love of enemies, to do good to those who hate Christians. It is utterly politically incorrect to even mention these *Quranic* passages from the *Quran and Haddith* (the holy books of Islam) calling for the death of Jews and Christians. It is here that we find the source of violence against Christians and no where else. It is utterly politically incorrect to say this by the media in the West for fear of being branded 'Islamaphobia' or 'racist' - and perhaps as an incitement to violence by Muslims. Muslim children from the time of infancy are taught to hate infidel Christians and Jews. In fact, the very prayer that every Muslim recites five times a day contains hatred of Christians and Jews. It is here in the education of the young and passages from the *Quran* that we find the incubators of hate and violence against Christians. No such hatred of Muslims is ever taught in western schools. Here is the factual record of the Islamic war on Christians in several different countries over the past twenty years:

– Chaldean Catholic Christians in Iraq are murdered in their own church during Mass, killing scores by Islamic self bombers. They have had to abandon Iraq *en masse*.

– Coptic Christians in Egypt have been persecuted and murdered by Muslims for years and their churches burned which they are not even permitted to rebuild or repair.

– In the Philippines south, whole war by Muslims has been declared on Christians, murdering scores in villages throughout the south and capturing still others for ransom. Their objective is an establishment of an Islamic republic in south Philippines.

– Turkey after the Armenian holocaust has severely restricted Orthodox Christians and its patriarch. Christians are murdered on a constant basis in that country in spite of the fact that it is supposed to be secular.

– Christian converts from Islam are threatened with death in Afghanistan by Muslims. A mob of Muslims killed thirty innocent people to avenge the burning of the *Quran* in Florida.

– Christians in Indonesia have their homes and churched burned down by Muslim mobs who have killed scores of Christians.

– In Nigeria, thousands of Christians have been killed by Muslims.

– Perhaps as many as two million Christians and Animists have been killed in southern Sudan for refusing to live by *sharia* Islamic law. Millions more are in exile.

– In Iran, the Christian community has been wiped out by murder and persecution along with non Islamic religious sects.

– In Lebanon, the Maronite community has been attacked, its members murdered so that very many have had to move to the United States or South America.

– Christians were murdered in Bali (Australians) by the hundreds by Islamic terrorists.

– Christians in Pakistan are murdered in their churches and many more imprisoned by Muslims under blasphemy laws which can be levied by one Muslim without proof.

– Eight Trappist monks killed in Algeria by radical Muslims.

– Not to mention the two million Armenian Christians murdered by Ottoman Muslims in 1915-1918. And much more.

What is wrong with Christians in the West who have not protested any of these atrocities against their fellow Christians by Muslims and only by Muslims? A burned *Quran* creates a Muslim mob in Afghanistan, killing over thirty innocent civilians when they couldn't find any Americans to kill. Muslims protest against a burnt *Quran* or a *Quran* flushed down the toilet (not proven) and some cartoons of Mohammad in a Danish newspaper, all resulting in the death of hundreds of innocent people by mobs of murderous Muslims; while not a peep from Christians in the West for the murder and imprisonment of thousands of their fellow Christians by Muslims all over the world. Hypocrisy? Double standard? Politically incorrect? Fear of further violence by Muslims? In addition, we hear not a word of protest by American Muslims against the atrocities against Christians by their fellow Muslims. Perhaps all these American Christians in the United States are too busy defending American Muslims from perceived discrimination while their fellow Christians are murdered by the bushel by Muslims the world over.

So we come to a stark conclusion: how many Christians have retaliated and killed Muslims and burnt down their mosques? ZERO. Now what would be the violent protest by Muslims if Christians all over the West and the United States invaded and destroyed mosques and killed thousands of their fellow Muslims? One can only imagine what would happen when they kill for a burnt *Quran* or a truth telling lecture by the Pope. But Christians? They have abandoned their own brothers and sisters in not protesting this Muslim evil all over the world. The war is a Muslim war on Christians.

# CHAPTER 24

# SOME EXAMPLES FROM THE QURAN

Perhaps the most despicable thing about the Libyan's Muslim woman, Eman al-Obeidey who tried to tell her story of rape to the international news media while she was dragged off by Quaddafi's security people, is that not one group of American feminists have come to her defense. Not a one. Rape is rape whether in the Islamic world or in New York City. It is a degradation and humiliation of a woman, anywhere, irrespective of race, color or religion.

The real problem of rape in Islamic countries is deep and unnoticed in western feminist circles because it is unpolitical coupled with the fear of being called Islamaphobia even in the American press. This problem for women goes deeper than nibab face covering - even though this too is a degradation of women. The problem goes deeper because it lies at the core of Islam's view of women and rape itself. It is because, in sum, Islam and Allah hate women and see them as simple birthers with no real personality and no individual personhood. More of this later.

When the *Hadith* says that a woman must produce four male witnesses to her rape, this insures that rape will never be reported or prosecuted in Muslim countries without her being branded as a prostitute. In fact, under *sharia* law, failure to produce such witnesses after accusation will subject the woman accuser to imprisonment and even to death by stoning. This goes on all over the Islamic world where women fear to come forward. They are continuously raped by relatives and others and they have no defense and the rapist knows it.

In addition, if a woman objects to the one proposed for marriage by her parents, she can be stoned to death. Even medical examinations exist to prove that she is a virgin for marriage prospects. If she cannot prove it (broken by accident, for example) again she may be stoned or banded as a prostitute.

When Ms. Obeidey tried to tell her story she was accused by the Libyan media of being a thief, a prostitute and other vile accusations for which the media did not produce a shred of evidence. The Libyan media simply presupposed she was a prostitute since she did not produce any witnesses to her rape nor did she cover her hair (only prostitutes do not cover their hair). She has been held in solitary confinement with no access to the media. Where are the American feminists? They have all left this poor woman at the mercy of a woman hating Islamic society. There of course is much more.

What is a Muslim woman? In Islam according to the *Quran* "a woman is a defect" and this has been handed down from the time of Mohammad. When Mohammad took a girl of six years, married her and consummated the marriage at age nine, this was simply and purely a crime no matter what the *Quran* says in giving permission for this. In this sense, Mohammad was a child molester. In another context, Safia Bint Hayi was a Jewish woman whose husband, father and brother Mohammad had been killed, finds herself in Mohammad's arms, married on the same day that Mohammad had killed her family in the raid of the Khaybar tribe. In fact, Mohammad gave permission to his men to rape women captives even if they were married. "Many women may seem good to you. Two, three, four of them" (4.3). No word on how the woman (women) feel about such an arrangement. Marriage is what seems "good" to the male without any deference to the feelings of the women. Women are a commodity to give birth and satisfy the lust of men with not a word of "family" with the equality of husband and wife and children. Children are property of the male and women are simple chattel.

In yet another passage we read "Your women are your fields; go then and do with your fields as you please" (2:223). The women is where you plant your seed for children and a man sows his seed wherever/whenever it pleases him. Women are fields for the pleasure and sperm of men. All is under a man's control and according to his wishes. Woman is like dirt to be plowed, seeded and produce fruit (children) and pleasure. Women are the dirt of Islam which men can trod on at their pleasure. The relationship is not one of love, equality, union in sentiment but a relation of a farmer to his land. In all this, Islam views women as defective beings and that is how they are educated. Having convinced themselves of their defectiveness, they view this as a divine decree.

Here is another *Hadith* from the prophet: "A man has the right to expect his wife, if his nose runs with blood, mucus or pus, to lick it up with her tongue." This degradation shows why women are considered defective when a man can expect such a degrading service from his wife. She is not his equal but his slave. Such a service is not mandated for a man to do. Here is another view of the Prophet in the *Hadith*.

> 'On the night the angel took me up into the heavens I passed by hell and saw women suffer all manner of torture and wept at the sight, so great was their torment. I saw a woman hanging by her hair and her brain boiled. I saw a woman hanging by her breasts and I saw a woman with a head of a pig and the body of an ass. I saw a woman in the form of a dog with fire going in through her mouth and emerging from her rear as angels beat her head with a stick of flame."

A woman who refuses to cover her head will be subject to such divine punishments, if she refuses to cover. This fear is from a sick view of the afterlife and it must be abandoned by any woman seeking freedom and dignity. A woman in fact who does not cover her head is regarded as a prostitute in the minds of most Muslim men. Hollywood has not come up with so grotesque a vision of punishment in any of its devil-possession films.

All this indignity heaped on a woman shows clearly the degrading attitude of Islam toward women. That such a God could do this to women is a clear indication that in Islam, women are feared and degraded even while American feminists turn a blind eye to what is happening to their sisters in Islam. This source of hate comes from the *Quran* and the *Hadith* themselves.

Consider Islam's opening prayer to be recited five times a day: a Muslims recites the *Fatiha*, the first verse of the *Quran* which describes Christians as those "who have gone astray" and Jews as "those who have incurred your wrath." These prayers excoriate Christians and Jews five times a day in the form of a prayer. Christians and Jews are cursed five tomes a day in Arabic. How can there be any possible dialogue with Christians and Jews if Muslims obligatorily curse them five times a day, each day for the rest of a Muslim's life? This prayer cannot change for Islam.

What kind of a God is it that uses the word "kill" and its derivatives some twenty five times in one chapter of the *Quran* (2:1-286)? This really is a God of hate for everyone except Muslims. It is in that light that all infidels are perceived. "Those who deny our revelation we will burn them in hell fire. No sooner will their skins be consumed than we shall give them other skins" (4: 56). What kind of a God could this be that metes out such punishment on those who perhaps through no fault of their own, do not believe in Islam? Is it any wonder that the followers of Islam often kill unbelievers particularly when they think that infidels have embarrassed, humiliated or even criticized Islam? They have been taught well by the example of their God. Among the attributes given to God in the *Quran* are the following: "The Hammer" "The Avenger" "The Compeller" on all those who refuse to believe. Such a view of God is degrading and hateful.

Fourteen centuries have not convinced Muslims that all these views of God are the reality of their teaching; that it is these teachings filled with hate and rejection, of violence and killing, *that have done nothing to improve their economic, political, social or moral circumstances.* This view of God has simply taught Muslims to hate and if possible to kill or at least distrust infidels. All the uprisings in the Arabic world for freedom will result in nothing unless this teaching and attitude of Islam are abandoned or severely changed. To return to *sharia* law is a sure source of degradation and backwardness in all these areas. The uprisings in Egypt, Syria, Libya, Bahrain and Tunisia are all uprisings for freedom. But there is no real freedom in Islam or *sharia,* only backwardness and violence. The Islamic view of the future on this earth is truncated by the Islamic teaching that this life is nothing and is only an entrance to eternal life after death. Only then will Muslims obtain fruits of plenty and joy:

> "Allah has purchased of the faithful their lives and worldly
> goods and in return has promised them the Garden. They will
> fight for his cause, slay and be slain" (9: 111).

The enemy is to be killed by the Muslim or the Muslim to be killed since this life means nothing; only to die as a martyr to be rewarded with all delights in the next life. Muslims are instructed to fight Christians and Jews until the last day. Hate will ultimately destroy us all as Islam destroys everything in its path. Teaching hatred of Jews and Christians can only lead to violence and death. If there is ever to be peace between Christians and Islam, this hatred must stop because it is a poison in the relationship. In fact, the whole concept of God must change into one of a loving Father of us all or there can be no peace as long as the God of hate rules Muslims. "Oh servant of Allah, Oh Muslims, here is a Jew, come and kill him" can never be a formula for solid ecumenism.

In fact, Islam if it is to live in peace, must change its view of God which is probably not possible. Muslims who live in America are truly torn between two views of God, of reality, of freedom, of the dignity and equality of women - all of which are contradicted by *sharia,* the divine law. I am truly afraid that there can never be true peace between Christianity and Islam because of their radically different view of God, of human rights and of equality of men and women.

All the uprisings in the Arab world will come to naught unless there is a radical change in the notion of human rights, religious freedom, equality of sexes, democracy and a respect of all religions. That is, if they do not submit to Islam and *sharia* that have kept them in social, political and economic bondage for fourteen hundred years.

# CHAPTER 25

# OBAMA'S SPEECH OF MAY 17, 2011

THERE ARE TWO ELEMENTS of President Obama's speech that must be faced and understood in context. The first element is that which is impossible to bring about in any Muslim country, namely human rights for all peoples: "We hold these truths that all men are created equal...." This is absolutely and institutionally opposed to Islam and denied by the *Quran*. Why then does Mr. Obama constantly insist on such an impossibility?

The second element is peace in the Israeli-Palestinian conflict. Given the same Islamic theology, this too is impossible. All Muslim lands - and Palestine has been under Muslim conquest since the eighth century - may never be given back to infidels. All Muslims are called to a holy war (*jihad*) until that land is returned to Islam. Only a temporary truce is permitted in *sharia* and that is what Palestinians call 'peace.' This requires the death of the Jewish state.

In addition, this much we all know: to reduce Israel to the 1967 borders is an act of suicide for Israel, even if you include "swaps." How do you defend a country which is at its narrowest is only nine miles wide? If Israel was surrounded by friendly nations, Israel could take a chance. But consider the changed situation on the ground. There are 300,000 Israelis with settlements on the West Bank and Jerusalem. In addition, the overwhelming numbers of Palestinians see Israel as an enemy and consider the whole nation as belonging to Palestine; Hamas vows destruction of Israel in its constitution which is now part of the Palestinian Authority; the same for Hezbollah in the north in Lebanon now supplied with the latest weapons by Iran who also has vowed to obliterate Israel from the face of the earth; if Egypt is ruled by the Muslim Brotherhood even in a democratic vote (one vote, then no vote), it wants war with Israel; with the Golan Heights, Syria could destroy all of northern Israel; repatriation of Palestinians into Israel would destroy Israel as a Jewish state; Lebanon is now controlled by Hezbollah from which all Christians are fleeing; Turkey is slowly turning to Islamism; and finally the "holy" *Quran* calls for the killing of all Jews. Israel is seen as a foreign body in Muslim lands which must never be given back to infidels (i.e. Jews).

To force Israel to return to unenforceable borders even with "swaps" is to ask Israel to commit suicide surrounded by haters who want Jews dead and Israel given to Palestinians. Muslim children are taught hatred of Jews and infidels from the time of their infancy. Obama has therefore thrown Israel under the bus by putting forth such a plan which can never be implemented. Finally, even if all these enemies of Israel succeed in destroying her, the small

Satan, there remains the great Satan (the United States) standing in the way of worldwide conquest for Islamic *sharia* which was/is promised in the *Quran*. *Jihad* cannot and will not stop with Israel.

The *Quran* which is the very word of God (*sharia* which is only its codification) demands the killing of all Jews whom it has called descendants of pigs and dogs. In addition, the whole world belongs by nature to Muslims which divides the whole world into lands of Islam and lands of war (not governed by *sharia*). There can be no peace until the whole world is under the rule of Islam and its holy law of *sharia*. Israel occupies Muslim land. It must go.

Now *sharia's* value system is diametrically opposed to our Judeo-Christian value system which is the foundation of America and American constitutionalism. Consider that eighty percent of Arabs in Arab countries want to live under *sharia*: no religious freedom; no equality of men and women; death by stoning for adultery and homosexuality; no separation of church and state; human rights belong only to Muslims not to infidels; *jihad* or holy war incumbent on all Muslims to bring the whole world under the domination of Islam and its *sharia*; no peace until the whole world is dominated by Islam and its holy law; death to all Jews and Christians unless they convert or live under *dhimmitude*; etc.

How then can President Obama in speech after speech preach human rights and freedom for all as well as religious freedom - since these values are only values of Judeo-Christianity, never of the *Quran*? It is a futile experience which can never be unless we change the character of Islam and above all of their vindictive, hateful, violent God, Allah, who hates all but Muslims. This is not possible so Mr. Obama musts stop preaching human rights and religious freedom to a people who not only do not know of these western values but desire in overwhelming numbers to be ruled by values in the *Quran* which are in absolute contradiction to our American Judeo-Christian values of freedom and equality of all human beings. This simply is not possible under Islam whose value system is not only contrary to our own but is commanded by its holy books to conduct a holy war against the nations which espouse these values in order to bring them all under the global conquest of *sharia*, God's law not human law.

It is more than amazing that intelligent men like Obama cannot understand this simple proposition: there may be some peaceful Muslims; there can be no peaceful Islam for the reasons given *supra*. We of the West are in a constant state of war against Islam which, according to the *Quran*, desires our conquest or death. No other choice is open to us except surrender. We therefore are at war with Islamic ideology. As to President Obama, one who cannot control his own borders cannot lecture Israel on hers. Our survival is one with Israel as we espouse the same values.

It would be interesting to know what American Jews now think about their seventy five percent vote for Obama in 2008. Obama is our Judas who is betraying the only democratic ally which we have in the Middle East. To force Israel to return to the 1967 borders or anything near that with "swaps," given all these mortal enemies surrounding her, is to destroy the whole concept and reality of Israel as a Jewish state in which there will be Holocaust II. Not only Israel but every thinking American must reject this latest call by President Obama for peace in the Middle East. Obama's speech was not a formula for peace but a clear formula for war. It is impossible for Israel to have peace as long as her enemies espouse the theology of *sharia*. It's as simple as that.

# CHAPTER 26

# ISRAEL AND THE PALESTINIANS: THE FINAL SOLUTION

THE TALK OF PEACE in the Middle East between Israel and the Palestinians goes on and on. Almost with the same solution but with Israel giving back more and more "land for peace" while the Palestinians give no real peace plan except a return to the 1967 border (not really a border but a military demarcation line). The most recent effort by President Obama in his May 17, 2011 speech for all practical purposes is a non starter. Any return to the 1967 demarcation line (even with the addition of "swaps") cannot really be a real start for peace. The Palestinians give nothing in return so that their intransigence is rewarded with new concessions demanded of Israel. There are approximately (in my opinion) eleven almost insurmountable obstacles to peace between Israel and the Palestinians. I list them here only for arguments sake. There are more but these are the principle obstacles for peace.

– Hamas, a terrorist organization, has joined into one Palestinian authority but whose very charter is the destruction of Israel as a Jewish state. How can Israel negotiate when a part of its adversary desires the death of Israel? That is a non starter which even President Obama recognizes as an impossibility for peace.

– Gaza was given back to the Palestinians in 2005 as a sign of good faith. Israel removed Jewish settlements from that whole area. The result? Rockets and death for Israelis in southern Israel. Instead of building itself with money from all over the world, Hamas prefers war with Israel. That is its very nature.

– There can never be a right of return for Palestinians which would mean the destruction of Israel as a Jewish state. Obama refuses to give assurance here - as did his predecessors. He now leaves it up to the two parties to negotiate. What is there to negotiate? Suicide? In addition, there is never talk of Jewish right of return to places all over the Middle East from which they were ejected at the beginning of the 1948 war for Israeli independence.

– Islamic theology means that land once Islamic (ruled by *sharia* belonging to Allah) can never be given back to infidels. The *Quran* stipulates a *jihad* for return of that land incumbent on every Muslim male. Even if it takes a thousand years. This is and will be a constant threat to the Jewish state of Israel because Jews are infidels who must be killed or removed. The *Quran* refers to Jews as descendants of pigs and monkeys.

– For three times before, Israel has offered the Palestinians an independent state - Gaza,

West Bank, part of East Jerusalem as its capital - in 2000, 2001 and 2008 and each time the Palestinians have walked away. How much more can Israel offer without self suicide?

– The Palestinians have never recognized Israel as an independent Jewish state - this includes Israel's neighbors. Israel is always referred to as the Zionist incursion or entity and never appears on the Palestinian maps. The vast majority of Palestinians consider the whole area to be returned to them (i.e. the destruction of Israel) even though there has never been a Palestinian state historically. Their children are constantly taught to hate Jews and Israel. There has always been a Jewish state historically in1000 BC, in 538 BC, then again as a recognized Jewish state by the United Nations in 1947. Palestinians have never given any peace plan except a return to the 1967 "borders." Palestine has never been a state historically.

– To return to the 1967 border is really an indefensible line. Jerusalem would be split from the Western Wall, from the whole Jewish quarter and from the Golan Heights which poses a direct danger to northern Israel. Israel would be reduced to a section only nine miles wide as indefensible. This would be absurd as a form of national suicide.

– President Obama has refused to offer any military guarantees to Israel for any final negotiated settlement with the Palestinians. Along with his refusal to state unconditionally against any right of return of the Palestinians, the promises of Obama's predecessors in this regard are null and void.

– Any "swaps" of land on the part of the Palestinians has been declared by them to be minuscule which means that the condition on the ground on the West Bank (now up to 300,000 Jews) would have to be uprooted. This Israel can never do.

– The threat of the Palestinians to go to the United Nations for a declaration of a Palestinian state along the 1967 "borders" will mean a further alienation of Israel from the rest of the world and the death of any further peace process since this would mean a complete repudiation of the Oslo Agreements between the two parties. Israel would then be free to initiate its own plan for peace.

– Most of the neighboring Muslim states are hostile to the Jewish state in accordance with the text of the *Quran* and the teaching of Islam. They really can't recognize Israel without really repudiating their own faith. According to the *Quran*, there can only be a temporary truce until Islam is powerful enough to eject the infidel from the land of Islam. Every Muslim male is dedicated to this *jihad* even if it takes a thousand years. This theology would be a constant threat to Israel unless this theology changes which is not likely.

These eleven obstacles to peace seem (to me) to be insurmountable. If the Palestinians go to the United Nations for a unilateral declaration of a Palestinian state along the 1967 demarcation line, this would invalidate Oslo. Israel would then be free to annex the whole West Bank. There can be no real two state solution and we might simply admit failure for over sixty years in all the peace "processes." Gaza can be given back to Egypt as a demilitarized zone as has been the case for the Sinai Peninsula for the past thirty years. Gaza has been part of Egypt for generations. Within the West Bank there can be a few self governing enclaves of Palestinians much like the situation of Indian nations in the United States: a certain number of recognized self governing enclaves which would be demilitarized. The Indian nations on reservations are independent and self governing. They have no foreign policy and are demilitarized. But they do govern themselves with their own laws and customs. The Palestinians will have the same right.

This annexation of course will mean further antagonism with neighboring Muslim states.

Even a threat of war. But with the West Bank in Israeli hands, the defense of Israel will be much more secure. The antagonism of her neighbors will be greater but what else is new? These states have always desired the destruction of Israel as a Jewish state. Now they will simply have another reason for more antagonism. The West Bank (Samaria and Judea) which were always part of historic Israel, can become productive along with the rest of Israel instead of the backward land in the hands of the Palestinians. The Palestinians have done nothing with that land for generations even under the Turkish Ottomans. Compensation can be paid to those Palestinians who want to settle in other Muslim countries such as Jordan, their real homeland. There will be no further immigration of Palestinians into the land of Israel now made whole by this annexation, thus insuring its continual Jewishness as a state. Such a move will make Israel whole and put a stop once and for all to the charade of a two state solution which the Palestinians have refused time and again for over a generation.

# CHAPTER 27

# THE MUSLIM WAR ON CHRISTIANS

THIS SMALL BOOK IS written to awaken Christians to the danger, a mortal danger which they face, called *the Muslim War On Christians*. That is because, simply, some Muslims are killing, imprisoning and exiling Christians all over the Muslim world in the name of their faith. It is their continuation of the violent *jihad* against Christians and Jews mandated by Mohammad himself in the *Quran* and the *Hadith* (the holy books of Islam). I apologize for the harsh tome of the book but truth is sometimes harsh to say and to hear. Muslims in America do not openly espouse this violent teaching because they are a small minority but when they become a majority (as in the case of the Islamic world) the situation may well be reversed in obedience to the *Quran* mandating the killing and persecution of Christians just as is happening in majority Muslim countries. It is in these majority Muslim countries that Islam is full blown and followed to the detriment of Christians and Jews everywhere in Muslim countries. The United States State Department lists Muslim countries as having the worst record of discrimination and lack of human rights in the whole world. In the words of the Catholic Archbishop of Baghdad in light of the refusal of the Iraqi government to protect Christians in that country, "We cannot live with Muslims." More than half of Chaldean Catholics who have lived in Iraq for two thousand years have fled the country for fear of death and persecution by Muslims there.

I do not deny that many Muslims in America want to live in peace and harmony and do not want to kill their unbelieving neighbors. That is because they are as yet only a small minority as in America. But even there, there have been case after case of American Muslims who have conspired against and attacked their own country in the name of their faith. The examples are too numerous to mention (at least twenty two incidents). American Muslims are peaceful either because they are small in number or are ignorant of the implications of their faith or choose not to follow its tenets or refuse to take them seriously. Still others believe that all this will happen only at the end of time which then becomes a theological belief harmful to no one. In any case, the *Quran* and the *Hadith* (which has the same authority as the *Quran)* and *sharia* (which is the codification of laws in the *Quran),* have some harsh and deadly teachings against Christians and Jews. Moreover, these Islamic tenets are in fundamental disagreement with the Judeo-Christian values which we enjoy in this country. *Sharia* and the United States Constitution represent two radically different civilizations - Christian and Islamic - which are incompatible. These values have to do with the following: the equality of women, secular law administered by an independent secular judiciary, separation of church and state, human rights for all human beings, freedom to believe, disbelieve or leave or join any religion in perfect freedom without threats, freedom to lead one's life in conformity to the individual's value system, the equality of men/women, homosexuals, etc. Yes, even the right to burn the *Quran* or the Bible or the Veda texts, etc. For each of these basic values, the *sharia* is in fundamental disagreement with American values. Both represent two civilizations - Judeo-Christian-constitutionalism and Islamic - which are radically incompatible.

The only possible remedy for this radical division between the two is what Benedict XVI is always preaching: there should be and must be no violence in religion. Only then can the two faiths coexist in this world without constant warfare. We can live side by side with each other only if we assure each other that we will not hurt or kill each other for our different beliefs, i.e. respect for our differences in religious freedom for all.

Alas such is not the case throughout the Islamic world today. And it is mostly a one sided problem. Islam or at least a good part of it particularly when Muslims are a majority, has declared war on Christians everywhere in conformity with the directives of the *Quran*. Even the daily prayer recited five times a day by Muslims contains a condemnation of Jews and Christians. How do you speak or dialogue with a people whose daily and mandatory prayer is directed at the condemnation of Jews and Christians? Everywhere in the Muslim world, Christians are being killed and persecuted by Muslims and we must understand why.

We see this everywhere in the Islamic world. Christians are killed, persecuted or ejected from fear in Iran, Iraq, Pakistan, Bangladesh, Indonesia, the Occupied Territories, Jordan, Nigeria, the Philippines, Algeria, Egypt and elsewhere. Examples in each of these countries abound. Christianity cannot even be practiced in Saudi Arabia and any Bible confiscated by Saudi authorities are burned or thrown in the garbage. No non Muslim may even enter the holy cities of Mecca or Medina under penalty of death and any Muslim who converts to Christianity (or any other religion) is to be put to death. Only in Israel are refugee Christians allowed to practice their faith freely. In addition, there is no example of any Christian or Christian groups entering mosques, destroying them and killing Muslims. None whatsoever because Christians are non violent who must love their enemies and do good to those who hate them. There is no retaliation on Muslims by Christians. Islam encourages the hatred of Jews and Christians constantly from pulpits and in the education of the young - all under the encouragement and direction of the Islamic holy books. If you teach and preach hatred of any group, this encourages violence against those groups. That is simply good psychology. Hate breeds violence towards the one hated.

Unless there is a radical change in Islam away from violence and hatred - above all a renouncing of any form of violent *jihad* - there is little hope of any peaceful coexistence between Christians and Muslims, between Judeo-Christian values and *sharia* values. Honestly, there is little hope for any of this because it would require a re-reading of the literal commands of the *Quran* and the mandate of Mohammad himself. It all comes down to these radically different values which are few in number but substantial in their definition: human rights for all, a God who hates all infidels and who encourages his followers to hate and commit violence in matters of religion.

Why is it so difficult for American politicians and liberals to understand the following statement: *it is impossible for a Muslim following sharia law to be a true American following the Constitution.* This is a basic statement which each American must confront and answer without being called an Islamaphobe. The two systems of laws are absolutely incompatible and cannot live together side by side in the same political entity, the United States of America. It was Abraham Lincoln who said that some 157 years ago which is just as true today as it was then: freedom and slavery cannot coexist in the same country. What Lincoln said then is just as true today when comparing *sharia* and the American Constitution. We cannot and must not in any way try to reconcile the two. *Sharia* is slavery while the American Constitution is freedom in every respect.

In sum, I do not seek in anyway to rouse Christians to kill Muslims or to deny freedom to those Muslims who want to live in peace among us. I only want to point out and warn Christians and Jews that Muslims are related to a set of laws and values in their religion which are dangerous to Christians and to our way of life. This must be resisted if they appear anywhere in the United States. This will require a constant vigilance that such laws or values have no resurgence in America. My book is a wake up call to this mortal danger which we must resist every time any of these Islamic values and laws appear among us. Does this sound Islamaphobia? Partially, yes. It is a fear of a foreign and radically different civilization trying to make a foothold in this country. This must be resisted at every turn.

# II

Whatever the Arab uprising means, it seems that it will create more sorrow and anxiety for Christians all over the world. Paradoxically, Christians had good relations with those being ousted - - Quadafi, Mubarak, Assah. If these countries are taken over by Islamists, the future will not be good for Christians in that part of the world. In fact, persecution of Christians is the measure of Islamization of all these Muslim countries, not of democracy as we know it but of a relation to *sharia* desired by the vast majority of Muslims in that part of the world.

There are secular Muslims in all these countries who desire a state of freedom similar to that in the West but they have little power due to the fact that their numbers are small in comparison with the religious Islamic forces who dominate the scene in all these countries. Democracy for these Islamic forces is one vote and then *sharia. Sharia* controls every aspect of life, public and private, with no real freedom for individual freedom and individual choices as in a true democracy. Power in these countries resides with the Islamics who consider liberal Muslims betrayers to the faith.

What do we witness in the Islamic world today? Consider about a dozen countries where Muslims are a majority (when they are a minority they claim they are a religion of peace). To start with, every poll taken in the Islamic world shows that about seventy five percent of Arab-Muslims want to live under *sharia* law not under western law.

In *Egypt*, since the uprising, there have been more attacks by Muslim mobs on Coptic Christians (about ten percent of the population) along with the burning of their churches. Christians under Mubarak were relatively free to practice their faith but if the Islamic Brotherhood assumes power, this will be very bad for the Coptic Christians because the

Brotherhood wants to live by *sharia* law. This has already begun in earnest after the uprising which overthrew Mubarak.

Some specifics. In 2010 Copts in Egypt experienced an unprecedented reign of terror. An Islamic *jihad*-martyrdom suicide bomber murdered twenty two people ad wounded eighty more at the Coptic Christian Church of the Saints on New Year's Eve.

In *Iran* under the Shah, who was secular, Christians and other non Muslim minorities fared well. When Khomeini came in in 1979 and pronounced Iran an Islamic republic, Christians were persecuted, their churches shut down so that there is hardly a Christian community in that country any longer. The objective of Islamics is to religiously cleanse the whole Middle East.

In *Iraq*, Chaldean Christians who have been there for almost two thousand years, have been attacked, their priests murdered and churches burned with the result that most of these Chaldean Catholics have fled to Syria and Israel. The Christian community in Iraq has been decimated by Muslims where the Americans and the Iraqi government refuse to protect them. The Americans were supposed to have brought democracy and religious freedom to Iraq. Not true. Power is divided between Shiite and Sunni Muslims and there is no place for Christians.

For specifics here, there are too many. *jihadists* bombed forty Iraqi churches between 2004- 2011 - seven on a single day. The worst was on October 31, 2010 when *jihadists* stormed Our Lady of Salvation Church and began murdering worshipers in cold blood. Sixty eight Christians were killed. *Jihadists* planted bombs around at least fourteen Christian homes. In Baghdad. Two Christians were killed and twenty wounded. In January 2011, *jihadists* entered Mosol's Rabi'a Hospital and shot Nuyia Yanssif Nuyea, a well known Christian cardiologist who worked there. Another Orthodox priest, Rev. Yanssef Adel, was murdered at his home by drive by shooters on April 5, 2008.

In *Lebanon*, Hezbollah rules and the majority of Christian Marionites are leaving the country because of the Islamic threat by Hezbollah who want Lebanon to live under *sharia* law. The majority of the population is now Muslim who in fact want to live under *sharia*..

In *Syria*, Christians have traditionally fared well because of the secular Assad who allowed religious freedom for Christians. With the uprising by Muslims (Christians have taken no part in the uprisings), it is difficult to say what will happen to Christians if Assad is deposed and Islamics rule

In *Saudi Arabia*, no religion is permitted except Islam. There is a constant search for subversive and hidden Christians in that country even as Saudi's finance mosques all over the world. Anyone who is not Muslim who enters Mecca or Median is subject to death.

In *Sudan*, *sharia* law is being forced on all residents. Christians and Animists alike. There has been a twelve year war with two million Christians and Animists killed by the northern Islamic army - and as many forced into exile in surrounding countries. Since the referendum of separation overwhelmingly passed in the south, there is great fear that the war will continue to force all inhabitants to live under *sharia*. The north Sudan has already taken over cities along the border with southern Sudan. This is the premonition for more war by Muslims.

The situation is fluid in the turmoil in *Libya* and *Tunisia*. There is disturbing evidence that radical Islamists are among the principle actors in the turmoil in those two countries. Christians under Qadaffi were mostly allowed to practice their faith. It is difficult to say what will happen if Islamism takes over the rule of these countries.

In *Nigeria*, Muslim attacks and the killing of Christians have increased due to the fact that their leader was defeated in a free election. They have rioted and killed Christians (and still up to now) since the end of that election because Muslims in Nigeria want all of Nigeria to live under *sharia* law. Two of the northern states in Nigeria have already voted to be ruled by *sharia* law. That is not enough. Nigeria must be ruled by *sharia* by the will of God. In Nigeria, Muslim mobs torched churches, enforced *sharia* codes on Christians and even horse whipped female Christian students whom they deemed inappropriately dressed. *Jihadists* have murdered eighty six Christians in bomb attacks at churches on Christmas Eve 2010. Two thousand other Christians were murdered in Muslim instigated riots in the city of Jos.

In *Pakistan*, Christian churches have been burned, priests and the faithful killed and most Christians are constantly being harassed by Pakistani blasphemy laws which are only a pretext for persecution. No evidence is needed except the word of a Pakistan Muslim. When Benedict XVI called for an end to this nation's blasphemy law, Fared Paracha, the leader of the pro-*sharia* party in Pakistan said, "The Pope's statement is an insult to Muslims across the world."

In *Indonesia,* there has been a constant persecution of Christians and a burning of their churches and murder of their priests and ministers in spite of the fact that the nation is supposed to be under secular rule. The government does little to protect Christians and often is compliant in the persecution when the army refuses to intervene to stop the violence. The situation was so bad that Christians in East Timor proclaimed independence with the help of the UN and the Australian army..

In the *Occupied Territories*, the situation of Christians grows more tense as many Christians have abandoned the land where Christianity was born and have left the area and have immigrated either to the United States or to Israel where Christians can freely practice their faith. Muslims have tried to build mosques next to the Basilica of the Annunciation in Nazareth and the Basilica of the nativity in Bethlehem to show the superiority of Islam. Israel has not permitted this fearing violence.

In the southern *Philippines*, bands of Muslim terrorists raid and kill whole Christian villages and hold many for ransom. They are fighting for an independent Islamic country in the south.

In *Algeria*, Christians have been marked for death by Islamic fundamentalists. We know that among the murdered were eight Trappist monks whose only fault was feeding and helping local Muslims - not conversion. Most Christians there have had to flee the country and go to France where they have a right of return.

In Afghanistan, a well known number of Christians must hide underground lacking churches and not daring to declare themselves openly as Christians for fear of arrest or death. The judiciary there upheld *sharia* law in condemning to death a Muslim who converted to Christianity.

These are only a few details of the situation of Christians in the Islamic world. Clearly then this is a war on Christians whom Muslim want to see leave these countries to declare them all Islamic republics. These are considered Muslim lands and the only right infidels there have is a diminished citizenship called *dhimmitude* as a submission to Islam. It is a vast effort at religious cleansing of all these Islamic lands to facilitate the creation not of democracy but of the califate or rule of the whole world under *sharia* under the successor of Mohammad. We must be wary of Arab uprisings that they not be taken over by elements of Islamics. This is a far cry from Islam as a religion of peace; as to Christians in these countries, it is a religion of war. Islam will not and cannot cease *jihad* until the whole world is subject and submissive to *sharia* or God's holy law. That may take a hundred years or ten thousand years, but Allah assures Muslims of ultimate victory. That is the kind of an enemy we are up against, one who will not quit until the very end.

Do Christians really realize what they are up against and the seriousness of their situation? I have my doubts.

# CHAPTER 28

# SIGNIFICANCE OF THE GUILTY SENTENCE OF JOHN DAMJANJCK

I WAS INTRIGUED BY the legal analysis of the German judges who convicted John Damjanjck, a guard at Sobibor prison in Poland on 28,000 counts of accessory to murder. The reasoning of the court was a form of personal responsibility for action which the defendant did knowingly and intentionally.

The defendant was found to be a guard at Sobibor death camp which exterminated 28,000 human beings, mostly Jews. The court did not find that the defendant had any hand in the direct killing of the victims. But he had cooperated in the killing because he was a guard confining the victims so that they could not escape. The court found that the defendant was fully aware of what the officials at the camp were doing and he did not try to escape. Others did escape when they found out what they were doing at the camp. The defendant stayed when he could have escaped with no harm to himself. There is no one on record who was ever executed by the Germans when he refused service in such camps. All this made the defendant an accessory to murder because he stayed when he could have escaped. His cooperation was vital for the running of the camp.

The defendant's job was to make sure that none of the victims could escape, thus forcing them to the fate which the camp had planned for them. In other words, even though the defendant did not directly participate in the actual killing of the victims, he was responsible for making sure that the victims could not and in fact did not escape. One is guilty of access to murder when he knows of the terrible evil being done at the camp; when he could have escaped but did not; who nevertheless continued his work as a guard voluntarily. Therefore he aided the objective of the camp and was thereby guilty as an accessory to murder. (The only surprise was that the defendant received only five years in prison with credit for two years already served.)

This sentence is noteworthy because it holds a person guilty when he sees evil and does not seek to escape when he can without great harm to himself, who thus voluntarily and intentionally participates in the evil work. Even if he was only a cog in these murders, as Arendt has pointed out, without the cogs the machinery of death could not function. Even a cog is a necessary part of the machine of death and could not work without it. That makes the cog personally responsible for what the machine finally does but not to the degree. Of those who ordered or did the actual killing. In addition, the statute of limitations does not and should not expire when it comes to the question of genocide or war crimes no matter how long it takes to bring him to justice (the defendant here was ninety four years old). All the ones who have participated in the genocides of Bosnia, Rwanda, Burundi, Congo, Sudan, Libya, Cambodia, etc. cannot rest easy for as long as it takes to capture them or as long as they live even if they did not directly do the killing but participated in an indirect way to that killing (e.g. guards, transporters, scribners, suppliers and all who knew what they were guarding, what they were transporting, etc.) when they could have refused to do so without great harm to themselves. Without each of these people, this terrible act of killing could not have been carried out. That makes each of them personally responsible if not in the active killing of the victims, then helping to facilitate that killing without whom the killing could not have taken place.

This is quite different from the trial of Ratko Mladic and Radovan Karadzic presently in prison at the Hague for the direct responsibility in the killing of eight thousand Muslim men and boys in Shebrenica, Bosnia decades ago. They directed and ordered the killing itself. There is no statute of limitations for genocide whether for direct participation or indirect participation as a cog in the machinery of death.

It is perhaps also true that these principles should apply to Islamic suicide bombers as well as to those who trained, encouraged and supplied them. And what of Islamic fighters who hide behind civilians or who fight from hospitals, ambulances, mosques, churches? The result is a direct and intentional killing of innocent men, women and children, which is a species of war crimes. That is why the nineteen hijackers who drove planes into buildings on 9/11 were not soldiers but criminals guilty of war crimes (if they had survived). No one doubts that if those nineteen criminals had had weapons of mass destruction that they would have used them not only to kill three thousand but millions. Is this not intentional genocide and their actions a form of incipient or actual genocide even if limited by possibilities? These nineteen were cogs in the Islamic war on innocent "infidels" which was part of actions intended to kill whole populations in America and in western society simply because they were not Muslims. This can be seen as solid and real steps toward genocide or attempted genocide. *Jihad* itself may be a war crime since its intent includes genocide of innocent people and as many as possible.

In addition, what do we make of parts of the *Quran* which calls for the wholesale killing of all peoples who are not Muslims? The threat to destroy Israel and all Jews in it by Islamic officials, are they not guilty of solid steps toward incipient or attempted genocide and should be charged as such? All this is like the allies in 1938 who refused to believe Hitler when he promised in *Mein Kampf* to destroy all the Jews in Europe - and beyond. The promised genocide is done by leaders like the President of Iran and by the holy book of the *Quran*. All this is preached and advocated each Friday from pulpits in mosques all over the Islamic world. Must we wait for the Hitlers of the Islamic world to consummate what they promised to do? These are credible threats made by people who argue from their holy books and whose only obstacle is their lack of weapons of mass destruction. Should we wait for this anticipated genocide on a massive scale before charging them with incipient war crimes or genocide? What of the morality of a preemptive strike before this genocide can be effected as a form of self defense? In the meanwhile can we not issue warrants for those who threaten such genocide whether from a holy book or otherwise? It is the holy book itself that lies there as an encouragement to war crimes and genocide. The *Quran* is an incitement to genocide. Given this credible threat by the mullahs of Iran, Israel is fully and morally in her right to attack the nuclear facilities in Iran which are producing the weapons of mass destruction which the mullahs have promised to use to destroy Israel. Must we wait for the strike which will then have been too late?

In any case, the basic principle of personal responsibility before a known evil when done intentionally clearly will depend on circumstances e.g. did he know of the evil, could the person escape without great danger to himself? how great is that evil? One answer has been given us in Damjanjck's case by the German court. This raises even more momentous questions which remain as yet unanswered such as the encouragement to genocide by religious leaders arguing from their holy books. Can religion justify genocide or war crimes? This is both a moral as well as a legal question. Our very future may depend on the answer to these questions.

# CHAPTER 29

# THE MOSQUE IN ISLAM

I HAVE OFTEN WONDERED why Muslims here and abroad want to build bigger and bigger mosques when the need of such mosques is not warranted by the number of the faithful in proportion to the size of the mosque.

We know that the names given to mosques relate mostly to the triumph of Islam over infidels. Thus the name of the mosque built in Cordova, Spain which was built on the site of a Catholic cathedral as a sign to the whole world of the superiority and triumph of Islam in Spain. That is why the mosque in New York City near the site of Ground Zero of 9/11 is to be called Cordova because, again, it marks the triumph of Islam over infidels as the nineteen hijackers had destroyed the very emblem of the infidel's prosperity and power.

More to the point, why the size of these mosques? This is because the land occupied by the mosque now becomes the land of Islam taken from the land of war occupied by the infidel. The mosque is essentially a part of the *jihad* war in the West against the West. Why else are there some two hundred mosques in New York City alone when Islamic worshipers in that city are so few? The more mosques there are, the more of the infidel's land is conquered without a sword for Islam. Therefore the mosque is more than a place of worship. It has a political and social message as a form of conquest. It is part of Islam's expansion in the West. It is where *sharia* rules until the whole world is ruled by *sharia*..

Why do Muslims build a great many mosques? Why a great mosque in the City of Rome at the very heart of the infidel's religion and space? It should be remembered that during the dedication of the mosque at Rome, Pope John Paul II had sent his representative to the dedication. Upon meeting the Saudi Ambassador to the Vatican and Italy, the Cardinal congratulated him and asked when would Saudi Arabia permit a corresponding Christian church to be built in Riyadh. The Saudi Ambassador was silent because he knew that any such event is impossible. There is little if any reciprocity between a Christian church in Riyadh (an impossibility) and a mosque built anywhere in Europe and in America (religious freedom in the West). The Vatican representative understood nothing of this Islamic theology and of the theology of the mosque. The mosque has both a spiritual and a political meaning since Islam is one reality with no separation of church and state. The church is exclusively a place of worship separate from politics.

In the United States there are over 2500 mosques for comparatively few Muslims of less than two million. You never hear of a mosque being abandoned once built or occupied (as is the case with Christian churches which are sometimes sold for lack of worshipers). Why? Because it is now a part of the land of Islam within the land of the infidel liberated by Islam which can never be given back or even sold to the infidel. The only time when mosques and the land of Islam is given back to the infidel is by the superior force of the infidel (e.g. Sicily, Spain, Israel, etc.). That was the case when Isabel and Ferdinand in Spain expelled all the "Moors" (as Muslims were called then) in 1492. The late Bin Laden complained bitterly about this and urged his followers to *jihad* to take them back from Spain, Israel, Sicily and southern Italy. That is also the reason why Israel is so much at the heart of Muslim preoccupation - besides the numerous condemnations of Jews in the *Quran* and by Mohammad who called Jews descendants of pigs and monkeys. Why? because Jews have taken Muslim land form the land of Islam by Jewish infidels. This land must be taken back as part of the perpetual war (*jihad*) against the infidel. In fact there can be no peace until the whole world submits to the law of God (*sharia* which is only the codification of the *Quran*). In other words, the bigger the mosque, the more land is taken from the infidel and becomes part of the land of Islam ruled by God's holy law.

That sacred territory of the land of Islam is shown by the fact that shoes are to be removed before entrance to any mosque. Even Pope Benedict XVI had to remove his shoes when he visited the mosque in Syria. The mosque has now become holy ground much like when God addressed Moses from the burning bush in *Exodus* to remove his shoes because he was now walking on sacred ground. In Islam shoes walk in filth or on infidel land which is the reason for their removal. Mohammad simply took this passage from *Exodus* and applied it to all mosques. The mosque is holy ground because it is the land of Islam consecrated to God and that is why that land can never be given back to the infidel. That is also why there can never be peace between Islam/Israel as long as Israel exists on stolen land occupying the land of Islam. This will always be a threat to Israel's existence

This theology is replicated everywhere where Muslims conquer infidel territory and made it the land of Islam and dedicated to God and God's holy law. Muslims built their mosques over infidels' holy places or very near to them to show Islam's superiority. That is to show the superiority of Islam over all religions particularly over its arch-rival, Christianity. Here are some examples:

– *In 1452 after the conquest of Constantinople* by Muslim armies the city was renamed Istanbul. More to the point, the great church of Orthodox Christianity, Santa Sophia, was turned into a mosque now with four added minarets around it.

– *No church of any other religion than Islam* may be permitted in Saudi Arabia. The holy cities of Mecca and Medina are forbidden entrance by infidels under penalty of death.

– *The Mosque of the Dome of the Rock in Jerusalem* is built directly over the once Jewish Temple of Solomon. Only part of the Western Wall is still intact where Jews come to worship.

– *The mosque in Cordova, Spain* was built over a Catholic cathedral which marked the triumph of Islam over Catholic Spain.

– *The desired mosque in New York City* near the site of 9/11 called Cordova will celebrate the victory of Muslim martyrs who destroyed the very buildings representing the great economic force of the infidel. This mosque is seen by Muslims all over the world as a triumph for Islam. That is why it is so fiercely resisted in the United States.

– *The attempt to build a mosque next to the Basilica of the Annunciation in Nazareth, Israel* where the conception of Jesus took place but was rejected by the Israeli government as well as a *mosque next to the Basilica of the Nativity* where Christ was born. This too was rejected by the Israeli government for fear of violence.

 – *The very large mosque built at Rome, Italy* near the Vatican to once again show the superiority of Islam over the Catholic Church.

 – *The ten thousand mosques built in Europe* and the two thousand in the United States for the reasons stated *supra*. All this does not include the thousands of mosques built all over the non Islamic world by Saudi petroleum money.

Thus the mosque is not simply a building where Muslims go to worship and to hear the word of God. Above all it has an inherent religious meaning beyond just worship. Since there is no separation of Church and state in Islam, the religious and the political are one - unlike Christianity which separates the two powers. The mosque above all is a sign of triumph and exaltation of Islam here and all over the world. Each mosque built in and over the territory of the infidel is an extension of Islam's conquest to be ruled by God's holy law of *sharia*. As Muslims become more numerous and more powerful, they will insist more and more on Islamic traditions and times and places of worship until they are strong enough to impose *sharia* throughout the lands of the infidel to become the land of Islam where only God's law will rule. The *Quran* permits a temporary truce when Islam is weak until it is strong enough (*jihad*) to overpower the infidel.

As one author put it, "The mosque is not only a place to pray but a public and social space, a center for political and cultural propaganda - a reflection of the total vision of Islam which ignores the western distinction between the spiritual order and the civil and social dimension." Even more to the point are the words of Mohammad himself, "The whole earth is a mosque." Each mosque in Europe and America is a little extension of that theology in the lands of the infidel. The mosque in the West is a form of non violent Islamization to which all Muslims are dedicated.

# CHAPTER 30

# ISLAM AND CHRISTIANITY: A DIALOGUE?

I AM IN A quandary. I really do want to live in peace with Muslims but I am deeply taken aback when I read some of the basic teachings of Islam in the *Quran* and in the sayings of Mohammad (*Hadith*). I have come to two firm conclusions. There must be no violence in religion and each religion must be free to exist in every way: life, worship, expression, conversion. Without those two categories or truths, I fail to see any possible dialogue between Islam and Christianity. The proof of this is that none of this is present in any Muslim country in the world which has assiduously tried to simply oust or persecute what few Christians remain in that part of the world. When Muslims come to these shores they have complete freedom to preach, teach, build all the while giving lip service to freedom - even in light of example after example of American Muslims turning against their own country. When we in the West point out this situation of non freedom throughout the Muslim world, we are accused of intolerance, racism or Islamaphobia.

The truth of the matter is that ecumenical dialogue is very difficult with Muslims as long as they believe in *sharia* which is mandated in Islam to govern the whole earth and infidels are either to be killed, converted or subjugated as *dhimmitude*. This Islamic view of reality is totally unacceptable for any rational dialogue. The dialogue must be a dialogue in reference to these basic teachings of Islam from the *Quran* and the *Hadith*. Muslims must not be allowed to wiggle away from explaining what this means and our freedom viewed simply as a temporary truce until they are able to impose *sharia* on the whole world. Do they really believe in *sharia* or not? That must be debated or the dialogue is useless.

Let me give an example from among many. Secretary of Defense Gates gave a speech to NATO complaining of the unwillingness of European member nations to actually fight in Afghanistan (they are mostly only support troops) and a constant diminishment of their military budget so that it is now the United States which bears seventy five percent of NATO's costs. The Secretary gave no reason why this is so. In reality, European nations have long since lost the foundation of their culture, i.e. its Judeo-Christian foundation for which their ancestors for generations fought to preserve from an Islamic takeover: Charles Martel in 732, Urban II in 1095, King Richard the Lionhearted and the Crusaders, 1100-1300, Polish King Sobieski in 1680, the Allies in 1915-1918 who finally defeated the Ottomans. Their ancestors knew what they were fighting for - preservation of the West and its Judeo-Christian values - and whom they were fighting against - Islamic conquest from the East. European nations have lost this patrimony (they even refused to put their debt to Judeo-Christianity in their new constitution) and what is there now to fight for? They are now more interested in economic benefits from the state to live comfortable lives by lessening their military budgets. In addition, they have admitted into their countries millions of Muslims who refuse to be integrated into the values of the West. What for? Europeans don't even believe in their own foundational values. Why should Muslims be integrated into them? Instead, Muslims desire to live according to Muslim values (separation of sexes, *sharia,* polygamy, separate from the rest of the population). Both the German Chancellor Merkel and the French President Sarkozy have publicly admitted that multiculturalism in their countries is a failure. In other words, Muslims have refused to integrate but prefer to live apart with their own values. Now all this is happening in nations that for centuries resisted Muslim invasion and conquest. The new Europe welcomes all this subversion of themselves without firing a shot. Secretary Gates sees the problem but does not realize the reason for the problem. The reason is simple: Europeans have nothing to fight for except economic benefits because they have lost their spiritual roots.

What is happening in Europe is ever so slightly being attempted in America. We can see the initial demands of Islamization right here in the United States: foot baths in public places at public expense, separation of the sexes in public areas, their own schools whose curriculum is not shown to the state, polygamy in certain areas, cliterectomy on the young girls, betrayal of the United States by some Muslim American citizens in growing numbers, distinct dress for women, demands for prayer time and other accommodations in public schools and private industry and no integration into American values. What we in America must demand is that there be no special accommodation for Muslims any more than for other religions. In other words, we must not become Europe or certainly not the darkness of non-freedom of the Muslim world.

As I have said, I want to live in peace with Muslims but only under the two conditions which I mentioned: no violence in religion and mutual freedom of worship in every respect on both sides. And these are basic rights, not temporary truces until Muslims are strong enough to impose *sharia* on all.

We can begin to see this in Egypt. What started as an uprising for freedom in every respect is being used by Islamic fundamentalists to persecute, kill and attack Christian minorities (Copts) in that country. And like Iraq after Americans spent billions and its life blood to free Iraq from tyranny, Islamic fundamentalists are now killing Christians and burning down their churches. Most Chaldean Christians who have been in Iraq for two thousand years are now forced to abandon their homeland. Everywhere in the Muslim world there is a war on Christians. For true dialogue with Muslims, this must stop. There is not one Islam here and another abroad. They both have their roots in the *Quran.*

Now we in America are called upon to be tolerant of Muslims when Muslims are persecuting, killing and ousting our fellow Christians all over the world. This is a tough sell even when our own religious leaders call us to tolerance and mutual understanding. Tolerance and dialogue is a two way street and so far, Muslims are engaged in a dialogue of the deaf. Until the above two conditions are seriously adhered to by Muslims (here and abroad) there really cannot be a sincere dialogue between Christians and Muslims. Indeed, between Muslims and the rest of the world.

What can we do? To admit to the West Muslims who want to live under *sharia* is intolerable. That is inviting the enemy of equality and democracy into out midst. Such Muslims must be excluded, no exceptions.  Our liberal Americans will not allow this so we are signing our own death warrant in admitting them into this country. There is no reconciliation between *sharia* and American democracy. They are absolutely contradictory. Some day, some how, Americans will have to choose and act before it is too late.

# EPILOGUE

This small book is written to awaken Christians to the danger, a mortal danger which they face. That is because, simply, some Muslims are killing, imprisoning and exiling Christians all over the Muslim world in the name of their faith. It is their continuation of the violent *jihad* against Christians and Jews mandated by Mohammad himself in the *Quran* and the *Hadith* (the holy books of Islam). I apologize for the harsh tome of the book but truth is sometimes harsh to say and to hear. Muslims in America do not openly espouse this violent teaching because they are a small minority but when they become a majority (as in the case of the Islamic world) the situation may well be reversed in obedience to the *Quran* mandating the killing and persecution of Christians just as is happening in majority Muslim countries. It is in these majority Muslim countries that Islam is full blown and followed to the detriment of Christians and Jews everywhere in Muslim countries. The United States State Department lists Muslim countries as having the worst record of discrimination and lack of human rights in the whole world. In the words of the Catholic Archbishop of Baghdad in light of the refusal of the Iraqi government to protect Christians in that country, "We cannot live with Muslims." More than half of Chaldean Catholics who have lived in Iraq for two thousand years have fled the country for fear of death and persecution by Muslims there.

I do not deny that many Muslims in America want to live in peace and harmony and do not want to kill their unbelieving neighbors. That is because they are as yet only a small minority as in America. But even there, there have been case after case of American Muslims who have conspired against and attacked their own country in the name of their faith. The examples are too numerous to mention (at least twenty two incidents). American Muslims are peaceful either because they are small in number or are ignorant of the implications of their faith or choose not to follow its tenets or refuse to take them seriously. Still others believe that all this will happen only at the end of time which then becomes a theological belief harmful to no one. In any case, the *Quran* and the *Hadith* (which has the same authority as the *Quran)* and *sharia* (which is the codification of laws in the *Quran)*, have some harsh and deadly teachings against Christians and Jews. Moreover, these Islamic tenets are in fundamental disagreement with the Judeo-Christian values which we enjoy in this country. *Sharia* and the United States Constitution represent two radically different civilizations - Christian and Islamic - which are incompatible. These values have to do with the following: the equality of women, secular law administered by an independent secular judiciary, separation of church and state, human rights for all human beings, freedom to believe, disbelieve or leave or join any religion in perfect freedom without threats, freedom to lead one's life in conformity to the individual's value system, the equality of men/women, homosexuals, etc. Yes, even the right to burn the *Quran* or the Bible or the Veda texts, etc. For each of these basic values, the *sharia* is in fundamental disagreement with American values. Both represent two civilizations - Judeo-Christian-constitutionalism and Islamic - which are radically incompatible.

The only possible remedy for this radical division between the two is what Benedict XVI is always preaching: there should be and must be no violence in religion. Only then can the two faiths coexist in this world without constant warfare. We can live side by side with each other only if we assure each other that we will not hurt or kill each other for our different beliefs, i.e. respect for our differences in religious freedom for all.

Alas such is not the case throughout the Islamic world today. And it is mostly a one sided problem. Islam or at least a good part of it particularly when Muslims are a majority, has declared war on Christian everywhere in conformity with the directives of the *Quran*. Even the daily prayer recited five times a day by Muslims contains a condemnation of Jews and Christians. How do you speak or dialogue with a people whose daily and mandatory prayer is directed at the condemnation of Jews and Christians? Everywhere in the Muslim world, Christians are being killed and persecuted by Muslims and we must understand why.

We see this everywhere in the Islamic world. Christians are killed, persecuted or ejected from fear in Iran, Iraq, Pakistan, Bangladesh, Indonesia, the Occupied Territories, Jordan, Nigeria, the Philippines, Algeria, Egypt and elsewhere. Examples in each of these countries abound. Christianity cannot even be practiced in Saudi Arabia and any Bible confiscated by Saudi authorities are burned or thrown in the garbage. No non Muslim may even enter the holy cities of Mecca or Medina under penalty of death and any Muslim who converts to Christianity (or any other religion) is to be put to death. Only in Israel are refugee Christians allowed to practice their faith freely. In addition, there is no example of any Christian or Christian groups entering mosques, destroying them and killing Muslims. None whatsoever because Christians are non violent who must love their enemies and do good to those who hate them. There is no retaliation on Muslims by Christians. Islam encourages the hatred of Jews and Christians constantly from pulpits and in the education of the young - all under the encouragement and direction of the Islamic holy books. If you teach and preach hatred of any group, this encourages violence against those groups. That is simply good psychology. Hate breeds violence towards the one hated.

Unless there is a radical change in Islam away from violence and hatred - above all a renouncing of any form of violent *jihad* - there is little hope of any peaceful coexistence between Christians and Muslims, between Judeo-Christian values and *sharia* values. Honestly, there is little hope for any of this because it would require a re-reading of the literal commands of the *Quran* and the mandate of Mohammad himself. It all comes down to these radically different values which are few in number but substantial in their definition: human rights for all, a God who hates all infidels and who encourages his followers to hate and commit violence in matters of religion.

Why is it so difficult for American politicians and liberals to understand the following statement: *it is impossible for a Muslim following sharia law to be a true American following the Constitution.* This is a basic statement which each American must confront and answer without being called an Islamophobe. The two systems of laws are absolutely incompatible and cannot live together side by side in the same political entity, the United States of America. It was Abraham Lincoln who said that some 157 years ago which is just as true today as it was then: freedom and slavery cannot coexist in the same country. What Lincoln said then is just as true today when comparing *sharia* and the American Constitution. We cannot and must not in any way try to reconcile the two. *Sharia* is slavery while the American Constitution is freedom in every respect.

In sum, I do not seek in anyway to rouse Christians to kill Muslims or to deny freedom to those Muslims who want to live in peace among us. I only want to point out and warn Christians and Jews that Muslims are related to a set of laws and values in their religion which are dangerous to Christians and to our way of life. This must be resisted if they appear anywhere in the United States. This will require a constant vigilance that such laws or values have no resurgence in America. My book is a wake up call to this mortal danger which we must resist every time any of these Islamic values and laws appear among us. Does this sound Islamophobic? Partially, yes. It is a fear of a foreign and radically different civilization trying to make a foothold in this country. This must be resisted at every turn.